Daily Discoveries
for September

Thematic Learning Activities for
EVERY DAY

Written by Elizabeth Cole Midgley

Illustrated by Jennette Guymon-King

Teaching & Learning Company

1204 Buchanan St., P.O. Box 10
Carthage, IL 62321-0010

This book belongs to

_____

Cover art by Jennette Guymon-King

Copyright © 2005, Teaching & Learning Company

ISBN No. 1-57310-453-1

Printing No. 987654321

Teaching & Learning Company
1204 Buchanan St., P.O. Box 10
Carthage, IL 62321-0010

Before offering any food to your students, make sure you are aware of any allergies or dietary restrictions your students may have.

At the time of publication every effort was made to insure the accuracy of the information included in this book. However, we cannot guarantee that agencies and organizations mentioned will continue to operate or maintain these current locations.

Table of Contents

Dear Teacher or Parent,

Due to the stimulus of a high-tech world, parents and teachers are often faced with the challenge of how to capture the attention of a child and create an atmosphere of meaningful learning opportunities. Often we search for new ways to meet this challenge and to help young people transfer their knowledge, skills and experiences from one area to another. Subjects taught in isolation can leave a feeling of fragmentation. More and more educators are looking for ways to be able to integrate curriculum so that their students can fully understand how things relate to each other.

The Daily Discoveries series has been developed to that end. The premise behind this series has been, in part, the author's educational philosophy: that anything can be taught and absorbed by others in a meaningful way, depending upon its presentation. In this series, each day has been researched around the history of a specific individual or event and has been developed into a celebration or theme with integrated curriculum areas. In this reality-based approach to learning students draw from their own experience and understanding of things, to a level of processing new information and skills. Each day students can be involved in creating a web or semantic map with what they already know and then add additional information as the day progresses.

The Daily Discoveries is an almanac, of sorts, a 12-book series (one for each month) that presents a thematically based curriculum for grades K-6. The series contains hundreds and hundreds of resources and ideas that can be a natural springboard of learning. These ideas have been used in the classroom and at home and are fun as well as educationally sound. The activities have been endorsed by professors, teachers, parents and, best of all, by children.

The Daily Discoveries series can be used in the following ways for school or home:
- to develop new skills and reinforce previous learning
- to create a sense of fun and celebration every day
- tutoring resources
- enrichment activities that can be used as time allows
- family fun activities

Sincerely,

Elizabeth

Elizabeth Cole Midgley

Labor Day

September 1
(varies)

Setting the Stage
- Display pictures of people in various forms of employment around related literature. This will engage your students' attention in the day's emphasis.

- Construct a semantic web with everything your students think of when you say the words *Labor Day*.

Historical Background
The celebration of Labor Day was begun by a man named Peter Maguire as a day to honor workers all over the country. Labor Day is celebrated on the first Monday of September. It is a legal holiday (since 1894) that usually represents the end of summer fun and the beginning of fall-type activities.

Literary Exploration
Labor Day by Geoffrey Scoti
The Man Who Didn't Wash the Dishes by Phyllis Krailovsky
The Shoe-Shine Girl by Clyde Robert Bulla

Language Experience

• Let students brainstorm all the jobs they can think of in 60 seconds. Then ask them to put those jobs in alphabetical order.

Writing Experience

• Give students an opportunity to write their ideas about what we should do about our country's unemployment problem.

• Let students write from the point of view of an "expert" about how to do a specific job (such as how to be a grocer or a plumber). They should assume that others know nothing about their particular field of expertise, so they need to expla[in] their job in detail. See reproducible on page 10.

I'm an **EXPERT!**

My occupation:

Name: _____

Math Experience

• Let students estimate how many workers from various fields they come in contact with in the course of a single day. They can each add the[ir] number to a class graph.

TLC10453 Copyright © Teaching & Learning Company, Carthage, IL 62321-

Science/Health Experience

• Discuss how using our skills and talents for the good of others is important to our emotional health and well-being.

Music/Dramatic Experience

• Let students play Job Charades! They can pantomime various workers performing their assigned jobs.

Physical/Sensory Experience

• Host a classroom job fair! Set up various centers around the room where students can get a taste of several professions. One station could be a doctor's office where students take turns being patient and doctor, nurse or secretary; another center might be a bank with banker and customer; another might be a restaurant with waiter, waitress and customers; or a seamstress or tailor might have a center where sewing is done. Let students participate in the centers of their choice. Encourage them to contribute resources (such as a play sewing machine from home) to help with the centers.

TAILOR
Fix Its – 10¢

Arts/Crafts Experience

• Let students make a job chart of their daily chores such as the one below. It can be taken home so students can chart how they help the families. See patterns on pages 11-12.

Extension Activities

• Schedule your class to visit various businesses or places of employment and learn from workers how their particular work is done.

Values Education Experience

- Today is a perfect time to discuss the value and opportunity of work. Unless they are encouraged to have a strong work ethic, children do not understand that work can be an opportunity and a benefit. Discuss opportunities in America. Point out that most people are able to find work to support themselves and their families. Although students are still too young for employment, they can begin to see school as their "work" and take pride in a job well done.

Follow-Up/Homework Idea

- Encourage your students to express thanks to parents and neighborhood workers (bus driver, crosswalk guide, etc.) for the work they do.

I'm an EXPERT!

My occupation:

Name: _____

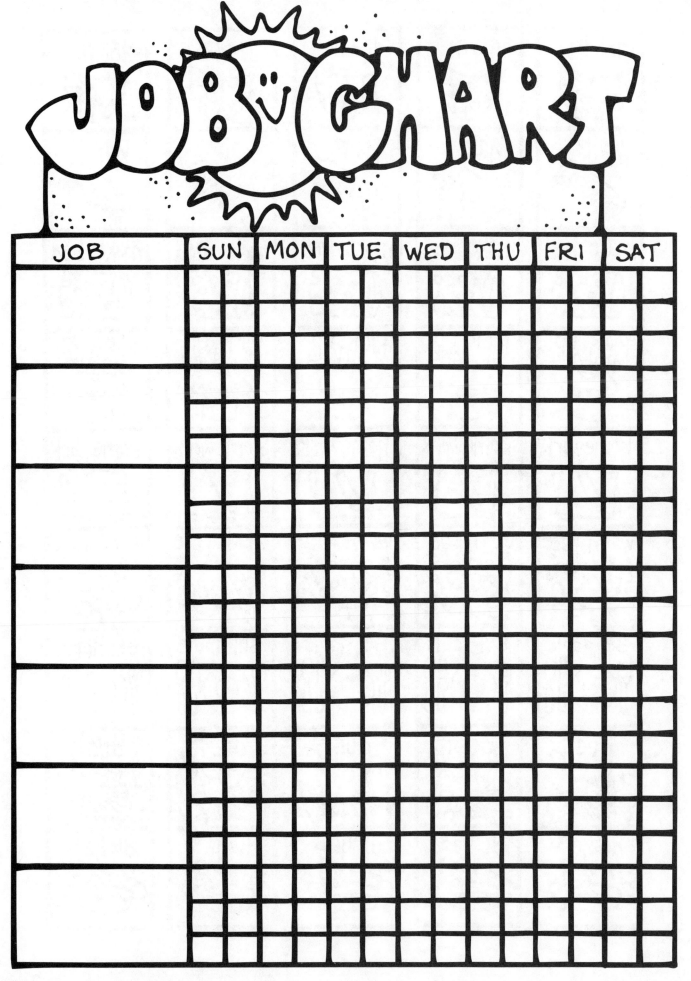

JOB CHART

JOB	SUN		MON		TUE		WED		THU		FRI		SAT	

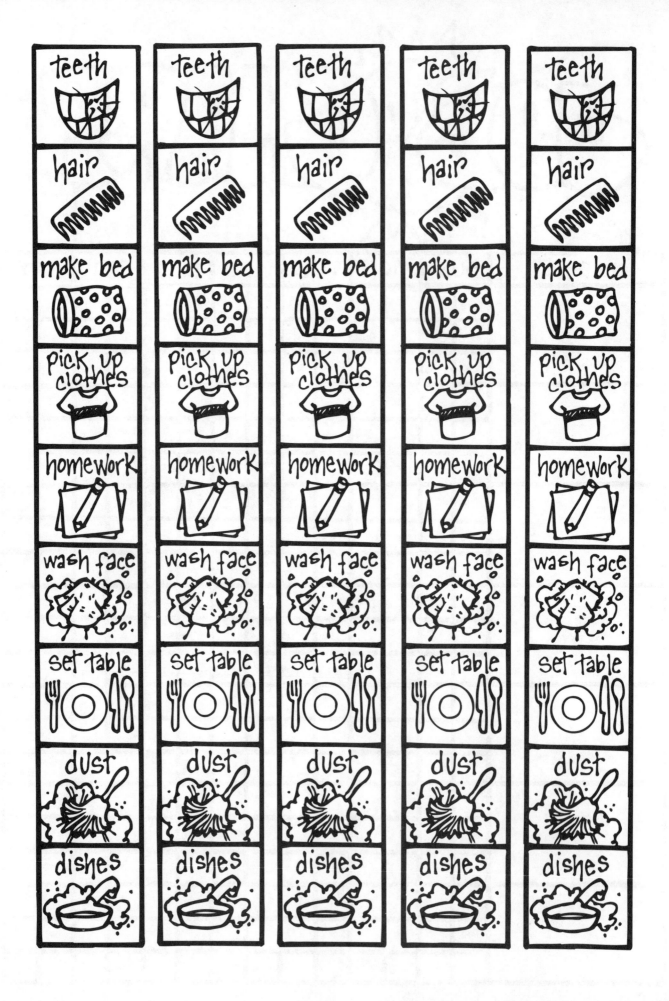

Lunch Box Day

September 2

Setting the Stage

• Display lunch bags, lunch boxes and a lunch tray around related literature to get your students excited about this day.

Literary Exploration

The Case of the Anteater's Missing Lunch by Vivian Binnamin
Cream of Creature from the School Cafeteria by Mike Thaler
The Enormous Crocodile by Roald Dahl
Feathers for Lunch by Lois Ehlert
Grandpa's Garden Lunch by Judith Caseley
The Great School Lunch Rebellion by David Greenberg
Howard and Gracie's Luncheonette by Steven Kroll
I Need a Lunch Box by Jeanette Franklin Caines
Little Bunny's Lunch by JoAnne Nelson
Lobster for Lunch by Bob Hartman
Lunch by Denise Fleming
The Lunch Box Monster by Carolyn Dinan
The Lunch Box Surprise by Grace Maccarone
Lunch Boxes by Fred Ehrlich
Lunch with Aunt Augusta by Emma Chichester Clark

Literary Exploration continued

Monster's Lunch Box by Marc Brown
Mr. Floop's Lunch by Matt Novak
A Most Unusual Lunch by Robert Bender
Munch Looks for Lunch by Keith Faulkner
Never Take a Pig to Lunch by Stephanie Calmensen
Out to Lunch by Priscilla Lamont
Out to Lunch: Jokes About Food by Peter Roof
The Phantom of the Lunch Wagon by Daniel Manus Pinkwater
This Is the Way We Eat Our Lunch by Edith Baer
Truffles for Lunch by Harold Berson
The Wacky Facts Lunch Bunch 100% Laugh Riot by Paul Zindel
We'll Have a Friend for Lunch by Jane Flory
What a Good Lunch! by Shigeo Watanabe
What's for Lunch? by John Schindel
Why Buster Beasly Was Late for Lunch by Teddy Slater

Lunch Box

Language Experience

- Let students brainstorm as many things as they can that rhyme with th
  word *bag*.

- Have students brainstorm all the uses (besides lunch) for a brown pap
  lunch bag.

- Create a class Venn diagram depicting the likenesses and differences
  between a hot school lunch and a cold lunch brought from home.

Lunch Box

Writing Experience

• Have students create an eight-line acrostic poem. Have them write the letters L-U-N-C-H B-O-X down the left side of their papers. Each line of the poem will begin with a word that starts with that letter. (Accept beginning sound for "x.")

• Let interested students write a (positive) thank-you note to the lunch workers.

• Let students write their favorite lunch menu on a brown paper lunch sack. See reproducible for writing activities on page 19.

Lunch Box

Lunch Box

Math Experience

• Let students take a school survey, by asking students (or observing and recording at lunchtime) who eats a school lunch, brings lunch from home or goes home at lunchtime. All this information can be put on a class bar graph.

• Let students practice counting money to give to an imaginary "lunch secretary" then trade roles to one who gives change for excess money given.

Lunch Box

Lunch Box

Lunch Box

Lunch Box

Science/Health Experience

• Review proper nutrition and explain the importance of eating a good lunch to help students as they participate in school and after-school activities.

Social Studies Experience

• Learn about what other children around the world do at lunchtime. Examples: Japanese children who have a "mobile" lunch brought to them on a trolley; European children who go home for lunch and children in South America who have a "siesta" (a nap after the largest meal of the day).

16

Music/Dramatic Experience

• Let your aspiring comedians tell a few jokes from Peter Roof's book, *Out to Lunch: Jokes About Food.*

• Borrow "Dirt Made My Lunch" by Banana Slug (a children's sound recording) from a local library to play for your students.

Physical/Sensory Experience

• Provide students with nutritional finger foods (such as cubed apples, cheese, pretzels, nuts, granola, fresh fruit). Involve them in their own lunchtime snack creations.

Arts/Crafts Experience

• Give students an opportunity to spruce up that old, tired brown lunch sack with a new designer lunch bag! Provide paint, markers, glitter or stamps and let their imaginations run wild!

Extension Activities

• How about ordering "in" today? Ask students to remain in class for their lunches rather than heading to the school cafeteria. They can have a picnic and eat their lunch on the floor or at their desks for a fu change. (Make sure this is acceptable to your school's administration

• Ask your lunch supervisor to let your class take a tour of the lunch facilities and observe some of the lunch preparation as it is in process

Follow-Up/Homework Idea

• Brainstorm a list of nutritious lunch items with your students. Make a copy of your list for each child to take home. Encourage students to bring a really healthful lunch for school tomorrow.

Name: _____

Animal
Antics

Animal
Antics

Animal
Antics

Animal Antics Day

September 3

Setting the Stage
• Display pictures of animals and any stuffed or toy animals you can find around related literature.

• Construct a semantic web with facts your students know about animals they might find in the zoo. Then have them write questions they would like answered about these animals.

Historical Background
Richard, the "Lion"-Hearted, was crowned the King of England on this day in 1189. Celebrate lions (and other animals) today.

Literary Exploration

1,2,3 to the Zoo by Eric Carle
102 Animal Jokes by Ski Michaels
African Journey by John Chiasson
The Amazing Things Animals Do by Susan McGrath
Animal Fact, Animal Fable by Seymour Simon
Animal Swimmers by Kenneth Lilly
Are You My Mother? by P. D. Eastman
At the Zoo by Douglas Florian
At the Zoo by Claire Henley
At the Zoo by Paul Simon
Baby Animals by Illa Podendorf
Bruno Munari's Zoo by Bruno Munari
A Children's Zoo by Tana Hoban
Dear Zoo by Rod Campbell
Do Animals Dream? by Joyce Pipe
Escape from the Zoo by Piotr Wilkon
Fitting In: Animals in Their Habitats by Gilda and Melvin Berger
Heidi's Zoo: An Unalphabet Book by Heidi Goennel
If I Ran the Zoo by Dr. Suess
I'll Build a Zoo by JoAnne Nelson
It Does Not Say Meow by Beatrice Schenk deRegniers
I Went to the Zoo by Rita Golden Gelman
King of the Zoo by Claire Schumacher
Lies (People Believe) About Animals by Sussman and James
New at the Zoo by Peter Lippman
Olly on a Safari by Teresa Frost
On a Safari by Roma Bishop
Private Zoo by Georges McHargue
Put Me in the Zoo by Robert Lopshire
The Right Number of Elephants by Jeff Sheppard
Safari by Caren Barzelay
To the Zoo: Animal Poems by Lee Bennett Hopkins
A Visit to the Zoo by Sylvia Tester
What Happens at the Zoo? by Judith Rinard
What Would You Do if You Lived at the Zoo? by Nancy White Carlstrom
When Water Animals Are Babies by Elizabeth and Charles Schwartz
Whingdingdilly by Bill Peet
Who Is the Beast? by Keith Baker
Wild Animals by Brian Wildsmith
Wild Animals of Africa by Beatrice Brown Borden
Wild Animals of Africa ABC by Hope Ryden
Zoo by Anthony Browne
Zoo by Gail Gibbons
Zoo City by Stephen Lewis
Zoo Doings by Jack Prelutsky
Zoo for Mr. Muster by Arnold Lobel
Zoo Walk by Greg Reyes

Animal
Antics

Animal
Antics

Animal
Antics

21

Language Experience

• Let students brainstorm as many different kinds of animals as they can think of and then put the names in alphabetical order.

• Create a Venn diagram depicting the similarities and differences between a lion and a giraffe.

Writing Experience

• Give each student an animal cracker. Let students make up an adventure story about that animal. See reproducible on page 26.

Name: _____

• Have each student write a letter to a particular animal in the zoo with questions to ask that animal. For example: "What's it like behind cage bars?" or "Do you like zoo food?"

Math Experience

- Each student can survey other students to find out their favorite animal at the zoo. Let them add this information to a class bar graph.

Science/Health Experience

- Today is a perfect day to begin a science unit on animals. Discuss the food chain, the interdependence between the plant and animal kingdoms and learn about the diversity of animal habitats.

- Let students research their favorite zoo animal and be prepared to give a short oral report to the rest of the class.

Social Studies Experience

- Using a world map, decide where certain animals are most likely found (such as monkeys in the jungles of South America, lions in Africa). Students can draw pictures of these animals, cut them out, then attach a piece of string from the animal to the continent where it is usually found. These may be displayed on a bulletin board.

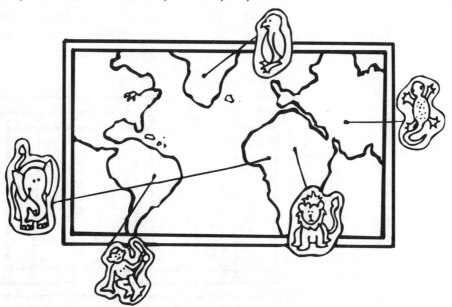

Animal Antics

Animal Antics

Animal Antics

Music/Dramatic Experience

- Let students debate the pros and cons of keeping animals in cages a[t] the zoo. Have both sides be prepared to defend their position.

- Any interested stand-up comics in your classroom? Let them try a few jokes from *102 Animal Jokes* by Ski Michaels.

- Have students experiment making animal sounds with various instruments: wood blocks for horses clopping, drums for frogs jumping, sandpaper for snakes slithering and so on.

Arts/Crafts Experience

- Encourage fast finishers to work on a class mural or shoe box diorama of the zoo.

- Students might enjoy making clay sculptures of their favorite zoo animals.

- Let students choose animals and make art projects by drawing them, cutting them out and gluing them on clean Styrofoam™ meat trays (from meat packaging). The top and bottom of the tray should have holes punched in—about an inch apart. Colorful yarn may be thread[ed] in the holes to resemble "cage bars" over the animal. These can be displayed in a miniature "zoo."

Extension Activities

• Invite a representative from a local zoo or a veterinarian to come and talk to your class about his or her work with the animals.

• Visit a local zoo for a class field trip. If you know which animals you will be seeing, create a Safari Hunt checklist and have students check off animals as they see them.

Animal
Antics

Follow-Up/Homework Idea

• Invite students to check out animal books from the library to take home and read.

Animal
Antics

Animal
Antics

Animal
Antics

ADVENTURES!

Name: _____

Candid Camera Day

September 4

Setting the Stage

• Display photos (color and black and white) around any related literature to get your students excited about the day's focus.

• Construct a semantic web of facts your students already know (or would like to know) about photography.

Historical Background
George Eastman patented the Kodak camera on this day in 1888.

Literary Exploration
Click, a First Camera Book by Robin Forbes
A Life in Photography by Edward Steichen
Snapity Snap by Stephen Wyllie
Step by Step by Bruce McMillan
Also, look for the photographic books by Tana Hoban.

Writing Experience
• Let students pick from candid photographs or cut out pictures from a magazine. Have them write a caption or dialogue between those in the photograph. See speech bubble patterns on page 31.

• You may prefer to have students bring personal pictures from home. Let them write about how they felt in the picture or the events leading up to it.

Social Studies Experience

• Louis Daguerre, an inventor and painter, is credited with developing a practical form of photography. As is the case for many inventions, it happened quite by accident. When a thermometer broke, the vapor from the mercury made contact with the silver plate and left a sustainable image on it.

Physical/Sensory Experience

• Let students take pictures with an instant camera for immediate photos.

Arts/Crafts Experience

• Students can draw "photos" (about 3" x 5") in a series, cut them out and glue them on a white sheet of paper (with space between them) to resemble a proof sheet.

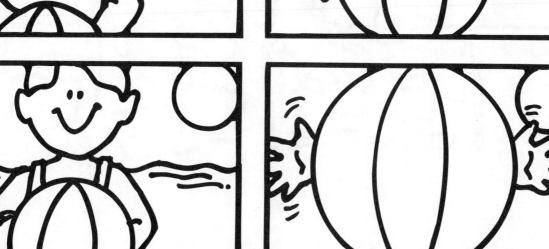

Candid Camera

Extension Activities

- Invite a photographer to come and visit your class to talk about taking pictures.

- Take a class field trip to see how pictures are taken, processed and developed at a nearby photographer's studio.

Follow-Up/Homework Idea

- Students might enjoy looking through old scrapbooks at home at some favorite family photos.

Duckling Day

September 5

Setting the Stage

• Help your students keep "all their ducks in a row" by celebrating duck all day long! Display pictures of ducks or toy ducks around related literature to bring excitement to the day!

Literary Exploration

Arnold of the Ducks by Mordicai Gerstein
The Chick and the Duckling by Mirra Ginsburg
Daniel's Duck by Clyde Robert Bulla
Duck by David Lloyd
Duck Duck by Edna Miller
Duck Takes Off by Susanna Gretz
Ducks! by Daniel Manus Pinkwater
Duncan, the Dancing Duck by Syd Hoff
Farmer Duck by Martin Waddell
Five Little Ducks by Raffi
Hamilton Duck by Arthur Gretz
Have You Seen My Duckling? by Nancy Tafuri
I Wish I Had Duck Feet by Theo LeSieg

Literary Exploration continued

The Incredible Painting of Felix Clousseau
    by Jon Agee
The Little Duck by Judy Dunn
Make Way for Ducklings by Robert
    McCloskey
Monty by James Stevenson
Q Is for Duck by Mary Elting
Quack, Quack by Patricia Casey
Quacky Duck by Paul Rogers
The Runaway Duck by David Lloyd
Stickybeak by Hazel Edwards
The Story of Ping (series) by Marjorie Flack
The Strange Disappearance of Arthur Cluck by Nathaniel Benchley
Swim, Little Duck by Miska Miles
The Tale of the Duck by Helen Cooper
Tale of the Mandarin Ducks by Katherine Paterson
There's a Duck in My Closet by John Trent
The Ugly Duckling by Hans Christian Andersen
Where's That Duck? by Mary Blocksma
Wonders of Rivers by Francine Paterson Sabin
Wounded Duck by Peter Barnhart

Duckling

Duckling

Duckling

Writing Experience

• Ask students to
  imagine waking up
  to find that they
  have webbed feet!
  Ask them to write
  about the adven-
  tures of their day.
  See reproducible
  on page 36.

The day I woke up with webbed feet

Name:

Science/Health Experience

- Learn about ducks and their wetland habitat.

- Let students experiment with waterproof duck feathers! Explain that order to stay warm ducks benefit from the oil glands on their back. The duck uses its beak to spread the oil onto his feathers (this is called preening) which makes water bead up and run off the feathers. Let students brush a small amount of vegetable oil on any kind of feathe (or other material). Then have them pour water on it. The water will bead up and roll off.

Social Studies Experience

- Locate on a map areas of wetland habitats.

Duckling

Duckling

Duckling

Music/Dramatic Experience

• Let any interested students act out scenes from *The Ugly Duckling*.

• Sing the traditional song "Five Little Ducks" with your students!

Physical/Sensory Experience

• Today wouldn't be complete without playing a favorite game, Duck, Duck, Goose.

Arts/Crafts Experience

• Let students make a mural of a wetland habitat (including bulrushes and cattails, birds, amphibians and insects).

Extension Activities

• Serve corndog "cattails" for a ducky wetland habitat treat!

• Invite a wildlife commissioner or local game warden to come and talk about working with wetland animals.

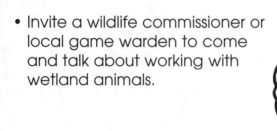

The day I woke up with webbed feet

Name:

Super Hero Day

September 6

Setting the Stage

• Display comic strips of imaginary heroes and pictures of real-life heroes around related literature.

• Have a little fun with your students by pretending to have a great weakness for books (as Superman did for Kryptonite). Ham it up every time you go near a book. Explain that you just feel pulled into that book and you must see and explore it! Your kids will never forget it, and the object lesson will be worth the dramatics!

Historical Background

Today marks the birth date of Marquis de Lafayette, a Revolutionary W[...] hero. He offered his services to the United States Continental Army (without pay). He was born on this day in 1757.

Literary Exploration

Balto the Hero by Angela Tung
Big Mose, Hero Fireman by Harold Felton
The Insignificant Elephant by Carol Greene
Maxi, the Hero by Debra Barracca
The One and Only Robin Hood by Nigel Gray
Paul, the Hero of the Fire by Edward Ardizzone

Language Experience

• Provide students with various comic strips depicting heros such as Superman and Batman. Let students read them, then decide what sets apart a real hero from an imaginary one. Create a Venn diagra[m] depicting the likenesses and differences.

38

Writing Experience

• Let students cut apart some comic strips, mix them up and practice their sequencing skills by trying to put the frames in the right order.

• Have students write about what they feel are the qualities of someone they consider a hero. See reproducible on page 42.

Social Studies Experience

• Invite students to research historical figures they admire (such as Abraham Lincoln or Florence Nightingale). Each student should prepare a three- to five-minute oral report on a person to share with the rest of the class.

Music/Dramatic Experience

• Students might want to role-play or dramatize something about their historical report figure or hero for other class members to guess.

Physical/Sensory Experience

• Play X-Ray Vision! Have all students close their eyes while you gently tap one person to leave the room and stay just outside the door. The remaining students try to see with their "X-ray vision" (memory) who is missing. Make X-ray glasses for them to wear as they guess. See patterns on page 43.

Arts/Crafts Experience

• Let students create their own comic books or draw a new cartoon hero.

Extension Activities

• Serve Super Cookies! Provide each student with a cookie, a dab of yellow frosting and a red candy worm. Students add a triangular-shaped mound of frosting on the cookie and then add the worm in the shape of an "S" on it! Remind them that even superheroes wash before eating!

Values Education Experience

- Discuss the value and importance of having heroes in our lives to spark our imagination and give us qualities to emulate. Talk about the need for students to also be role models and heroes for other people who may be watching their actions.

Super Hero

Follow-Up/Homework Idea

- Challenge each student to be an "unsung hero," quietly doing well and performing acts of kindness without fanfare or recognition.

Super Hero

Super Hero

What is a HERO?

Name:

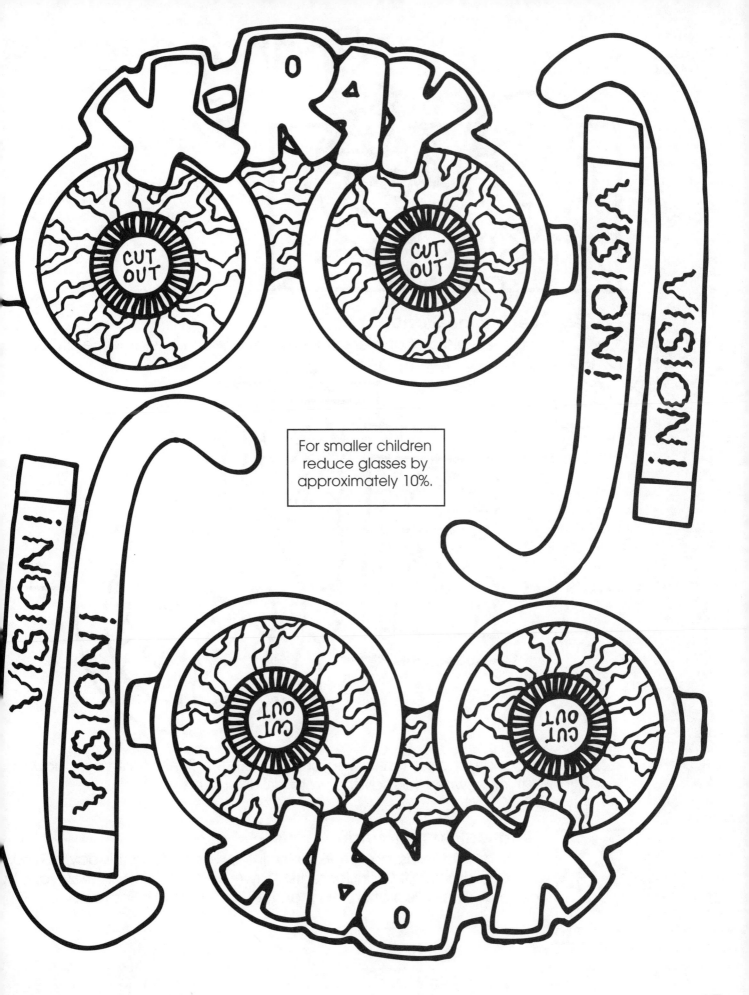

For smaller children reduce glasses by approximately 10%.

Grandparents Day

September 7
(varies)

Setting the Stage
- Display pictures of grandparents surrounded by related literature.

- Construct a semantic web or map with the things that your students think of when you say the word *grandparents*.

Historical Background
"Grandma" Moses, an American painter, was born on this day in 1860. The actual date of Grandparents' Day (from year to year) may vary, bu generally this celebration lands on the first Sunday of September.

Literary Exploration

Grandfather and I by Helen Buckley
Grandma Is Somebody Special by Susan Goldman
Grandpa by Barbara Borack
Grandparents by Maria Rius
Grandparents Around the World by Dorka Raynor
Grandpa's Long Underwear by Lynn Schoettles
How Does It Feel to Be Old? by Norma Farber
I Have Four Names for My Grandfather by Kathryn Lasky
A Little at a Time by David A. Adler
I Love Gram by Ruth Sonneborn
Just Grandma and Me by Mercer Mayer
My Great Grandpa Joe by Marilyn Gelfand
Nana Upstairs and Nana Downstairs by Tomie dePaola
On Granddaddy's Farm by Thomas Allen
Song and Dance Man by Karen Ackerman
Stone Fox by John R. Gardiner
They Were Strong and Good by Robert Lawson
The Two of Them by Aliki
A Visit to Grandma's by Nancy Carlson

Language Experience

- Review other compound words besides *grandma, grandpa, grandmother* and *grandfather*.

- Play the (alphabet) memory game, "In Grandma's Trunk."

Writing Experience

- Give students an opportunity to write letters to their grandparents. Ask them to question what it was like when their grandparents were in the same grade. Students should ask their grandparents to write back to them at school. Getting letters from grandparents telling what recess was like or how grandpa won the spelling bee will be a real joy for your students! See reproducible on page 49.

When you were young...

Social Studies Experience

• Illustrate how a "family tree" works (with generations leading down to the student). Let students create their own family tree with parents' and grandparents' names. See reproducible on page 50.

• Discuss what it means to show respect for the elderly.

• Invite students to bring pictures of their grandparents and, if possible, find out what country their ancestors came from. The pictures can be placed on a map with yarn connecting them to the areas of the world from which their families originated.

Music/Dramatic Experience

• Sing the old favorite, "Over the River and Through the Woods to Grandmother's House We Go!"

• Let students pretend they are up in "Grandmother's attic" by allowing them time to play with dress-up items (clothes, shoes, jewelry and hats).

Arts/Crafts Experience

• Let each student wrap a gift (a clay figure or child's handprint) in wrapping paper the student designed.

• Allow students to paint family portraits (including grandparents).

• Try this unusual way to display family trees! Students draw pictures of big trees and write the names of their families on the tree trunks. Then they draw pictures of family members (immediate and extended) on the branches of the trees.

• Each student can make a calendar and label a day each month to do something special for a grandparent. (Examples: weed the yard for nearby grandparents or make a long-distance phone call to a grandparent farther away.)

Extension Activities

- Schedule your students to visit a local geriatric center or nursing home

- Host a Grandparents' Day, inviting students' grandparents to a program of singing, poetry and refreshments to honor them. Invite the grandparents to share their experiences (as a grandparent) with the class. (Encourage children without available grandparents to invite a special person.)

Values Education Experience

- Discuss the value of learning from those who have gone before us.

Follow-Up/Homework Idea

- Encourage students to take home their family trees and fill them out with their parents' help.

Grandparents

Grandparents

Grandparents

When you were young...

Rockin' with Rocket Science Day

September 8

Setting the Stage

• Display pictures of rockets alongside toy rockets and related literature to gather excitement about the day's activities.

• Construct a semantic web of facts your students already know (or would like to know) about rockets.

Literary Exploration

The Magic Rocket by Steven Kroll
Richie's Rocket by Joan Anderson
Rocket Countdown by Nick Sharratt
Rocket in My Pocket by Carl Withers
Rocket Science by Jim Wiese

Writing Experience

• Students can obtain rocket information and pictures by writing to:

NASA
Audio-Visual Branch
Public Information Division
Code LFD-10
National Aeronautics & Space Admin.
400 Maryland Ave. S.W.
Washington, D.C. 20546

• See reproducible on page 55.

BLAST OFF!

Math Experience

• Let students play Rocket Math! They choose math problems (by level of difficulty) when they choose rockets from the bulletin board. Rockets with smaller numbers have easier math problems or questions and larger rocket numbers have more advanced questions. The student earns the amount of points on each rocket when they answe correctly. (A rocket with a "5" on it may have a problem such as 4 + and if answered correctly, wins the student five points. A rocket with "25" on it, may have a problem such as 5 x 5 and, if answered correctly, will earn the student 25 points!) Divide students into teams t play. See patterns on page 56.

See patterns on page 56.

Science/Health Experience

• What's National Rocket Day without a little rocket science! Explain that hot gases from a rocket propel the rocket forward. Illustrate this by blowing up a balloon. The air in the balloon acts like the hot gase When the balloon is released, it "rockets" forward.

Social Studies Experience

• Study the history of rocket launches and record them on a class time line.

Physical/Sensory Experience

• Let students create their own rocket demonstration. Give each student a straw. Have them thread a long piece of string through the straw; then stretch the string taut between two corner walls and tape the ends down tightly. The student blows up a long balloon and holds the opening closed. Another student helps by taping the balloon to the straw. The student holding the neck of the balloon lets go, and it rockets forward along the string.

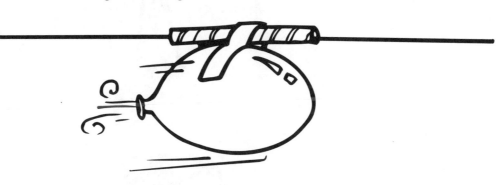

Arts/Crafts Experience

• Students can make their own paper rockets by taping an 8" x 2" strip of paper around a pencil. Tape it at the end to form a point. Students can add "fins" and decorate the "rocket." When your students are ready to "launch," they remove the pencil, insert a plastic drinking straw into the open end and blow. Blast off!

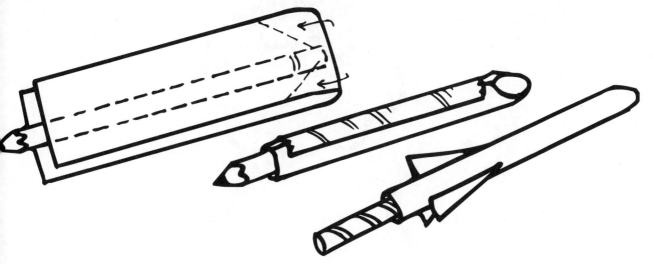

Extension Activities

• Invite parents who enjoy launching rockets to come and share their talents with your class out on the playing field.

• Make a rocket ship cake that is out-of-this-world! Purchase a jellyroll-style ice cream cake (or sponge cake) and stand it on one end. Add a sugar cone to the top and insert wafer cookies for fins around the base. Frost and decorate it to resemble a rocket ready for take off! Then eat it!

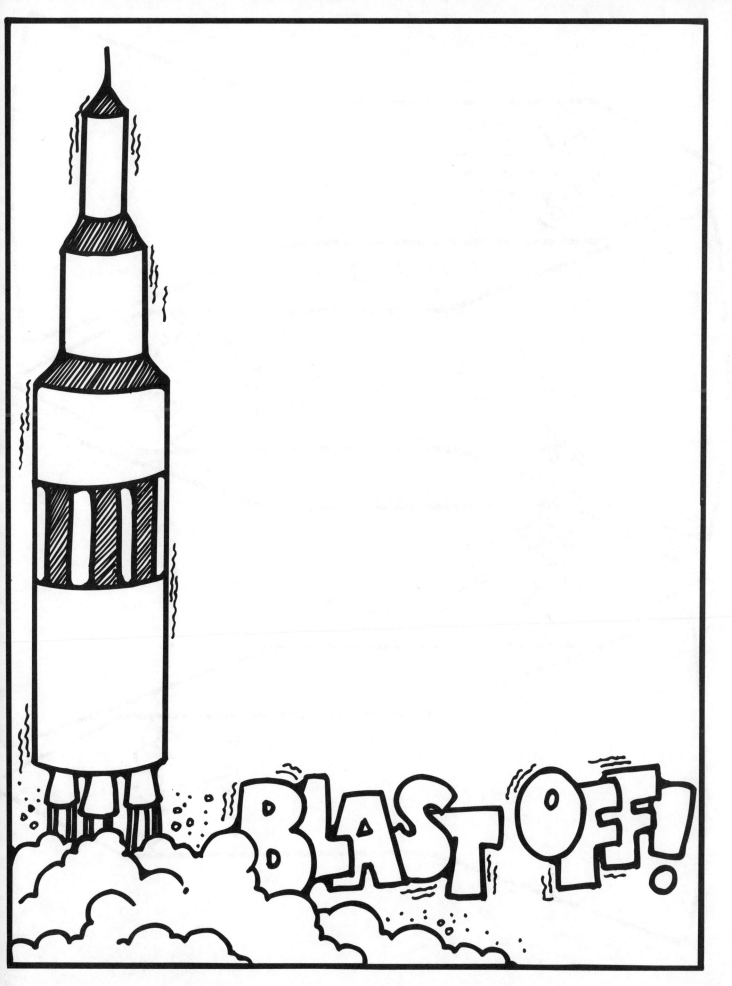

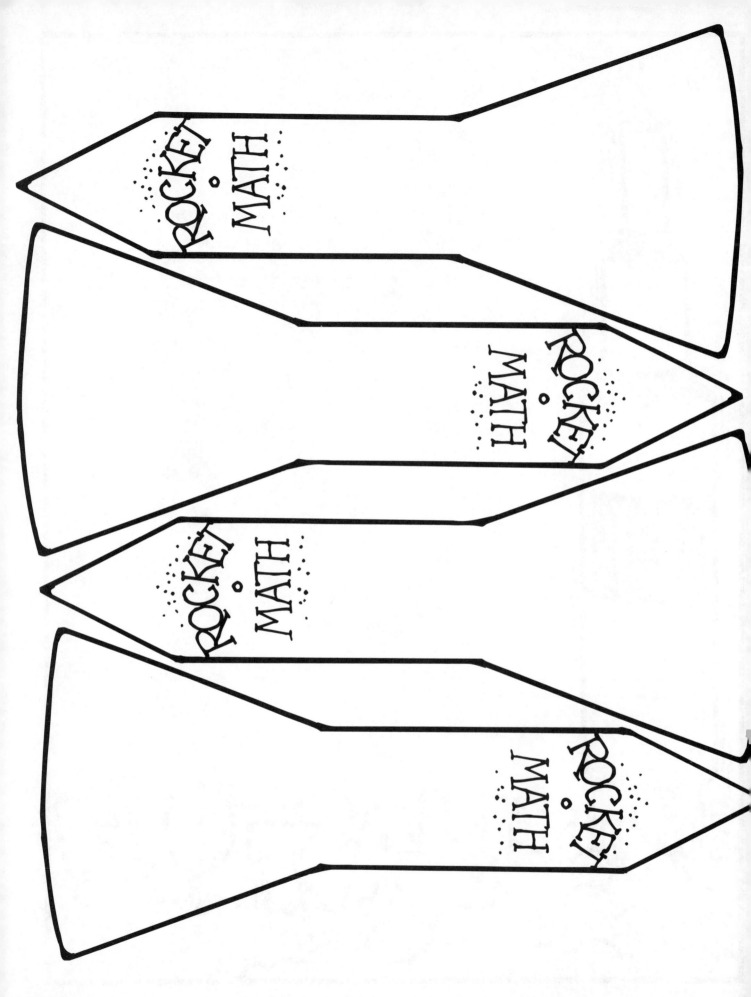

California Statehood Day

September 9

Setting the Stage

- "Lights, Camera, Action" or "Surf's Up!" No matter how you look at it, California is a fun place to be! Today your students will learn more about this "Golden" state and learn to appreciate one of the sunny sides of our country! Display pictures and other memorabilia (hat, seashells, etc.). Get posters and pamphlets from a local travel agency to display around related literature.

Setting the Stage continued

• Invite students to wear "beach wear" or sunglasses to get in the California frame of mind. Wear your own California garb and give instructions from a megaphone, just like a Hollywood director!

Historical Background

California became the 31st state on this day in 1850.

Literary Exploration

America, the Beautiful: California by Conrad R. Stein
California by Dennis B. Fradin
California by Janet Pack
California by Kathleen Thompson
California in Pictures by Cawley McDonald
Going Hollywood: A Dinosaurs Dream by Hudson Talbott
Picture Book of California by Bernadine Bailey

Language Experience

• Challenge your students to see how many words they can make from the letters in *California*.

Writing Experience

• Ask students to pick a favorite California destination and write about what it is like or what they think it is like. See reproducible on page 62.

Name:

Math Experience

• Since California is famous for the plump juicy raisins they produce, let students freshen up their estimation skills by estimating how many raisins are in a jar. Practice counting them (by ones or twos or fives) together, and see whose guess was best. Then let the student with the closest estimate hand out raisins to everyone! See pattern on page 63.

Just "raisin" a question:

How many of us do you think there are in this jar?

Social Studies Experience

• Study to find out what makes the state of California unique.

Music/Dramatic Experience

• Play a little California Beach Boys' music quietly in the background while your students work on their projects.

Physical/Sensory Experience

• If the Beach Boys' music gets them in the mood, let students dance!

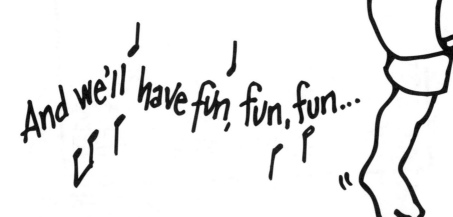

And we'll have fun, fun, fun...

Arts/Crafts Experience

• Students can be divided into cooperative art groups, each making a mural of a different aspect of California (the beach, a Hollywood movie set, the Redwood forests, etc.).

• Let students make a salt dough relief map in the shape of California. Bake at 300°F for an hour, then paint it.

Extension Activities
• Californians aren't the only ones who get to enjoy their chief product from the citrus groves! Serve citrus salad! Simply cut segments of oranges and grapefruit and add a little fruit juice!

• Invite someone who has been to California to share pictures and/or mementos from there.

Follow-Up/Homework Idea
• Encourage students to begin their own collections of seashells, rocks or whatever!

California

California
California

CALIFORNIA!

Name: _____

Just "raisin" a question:

How many of us do you think there are in this jar?

How many?

Name: _____

How many?

Name: _____

How many?

Name: _____

How many?

Name: _____

How many?

Name: _____

How many?

Name: _____

How many?

Name: _____

How many?

Name: _____

How many?

Name: _____

Diner Day
Sock Hop

September 10

Setting the Stage

• Welcome to the "Golden Oldies"! Display old 45 records around related literature to spark the interest of your students today!

• Encourage students to dress up 1950s style with bobby socks and ponytails, slicked-back hair and rolled up jeans! Be prepared to dress likewise!

Historical Background

On this day in 1927, the first hot dogs appeared in zipper casings. Do you suppose hot dogs were served at the local diner?

Sock Hop

Sock Hop

Sock Hop

Literary Exploration

The Ghost in Dobb's Diner by Robert Alley
In the Diner by Christine Loomis
Marge's Diner by Gail Gibbons
Mel's Diner by Marissa Moss
Mom's Night Out by Juli Barbato
The Peace and Quiet Diner by Gregory Maguire
The Robbery at the Diamond Dog Diner by Eileen Christelow

Language Experience

• Let students brainstorm food items that might be sold in a diner (such as milk shakes and French fries). After they have compiled their lists, ask them to put them in alphabetical order.

Math Experience

• Create a sample menu from a diner (hamburger $1.00, soda pop $.85 and so on). Let students decide the price of each menu item (what they think it may have cost back in the Fifties) and then tally the prices of various food combinations. See reproducible on page 68.

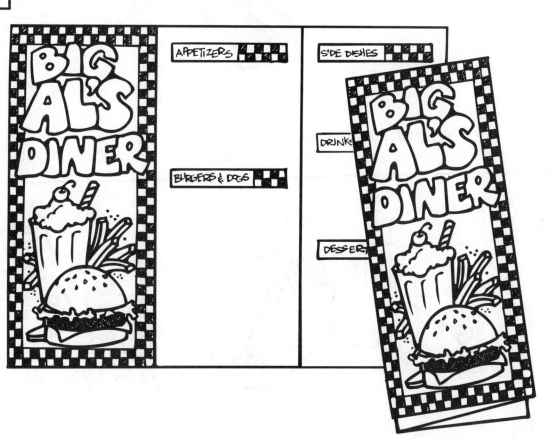

Music/Dramatic Experience

• Play Sock Hop "Oldies" in the background while your students are involved in their projects.

• A few brave souls in your class might want to try to "lip-sync" as one the "oldies" is played.

We're gonna rock, gonna rock around the clock tonight!

Physical/Sensory Experience

• Host a Sock Hop! Borrow some Rock and Roll Oldies from a local libr and let students dance in (what else?) their socks!

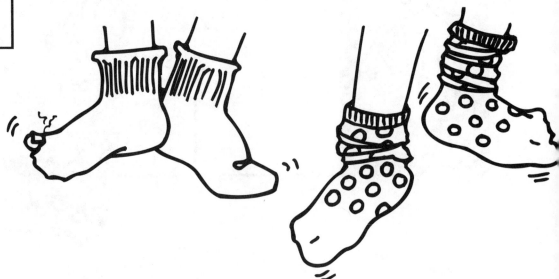

Arts/Crafts Experience

• Let students have fun with a little "pop art" by painting large pictures of hamburgers and fries, malts and pizza!

Sock Hop

Extension Activities

• Invite someone who was around in the Fifties to tell your class about that period of time with local diners and sock hop dances. Perhaps they have some memorabilia from that time period to share.

Sock Hop

Follow-Up/Homework Idea

• Invite students to ask their parents or grandparents about the Fifties.

Sock Hop

SIDE DISHES

DRINKS & MALTS

DESSERTS

APPETIZERS

BURGERS & DOGS

BIG AL'S DINER

68

Middle Ages Day

September 11

Setting the Stage

• Display pictures and books representative of the Dark or Middle Ages.

• Construct a semantic web with words your students think of when you say, "Middle Ages."

Literary Exploration

Adam of the Road by Elizabeth Jane Gray
Adventures of Robin Hood by Marcia Williams
The Castle in the Attic by Elizabeth Winthrop
The Door in the Wall by Marguerite deAngeli
Europe in the Middle Ages by Antoine Sabbagh
Exploring the Past: The Middle Ages by Catherine Oakes
The Knight Who Was Afraid of the Dark by Barbara Shook Hazen
A Medieval Feast! by Aliki
The Middle Ages by Trevor Cairns
The Middle Ages by Giovanni Caselli
The Middle Ages by Sarah Howarth
Robin Hood of Sherwood Forest by Ann McGovern
St. George and the Dragon by Margaret Hodges
Secret of the Forest by Neil Morris
The Story of King Arthur and His Knights (series) by Howard Pile

Language Experience

• Brainstorm other words that have double consonants as in the word *middle*.

Writing Experience

• Let one student serve as a "scribe" for another (popular in the Middle Ages) in a writing assignment about living in that time period, then let them switch roles.

Science/Health Experience

• During the Middle Ages many people in Europe died from the dreaded Bubonic Plague or Black Death. This disease was spread from infected rats. Discuss the importance of hygiene and cleanliness to prevent the spread of illness and disease.

Social Studies Experience

• Study the time period known as the Middle Ages. Let students brainstorm how life has changed since then.

Music/Dramatic Experience

• Borrow (from a local library) any music representative of the Middle Ages such as a minstrel's ballad.

Physical/Sensory Experience

• If you have access to foam bats, let your students try their hand at a little "jousting"!

• Teach students some calligraphy. Let them try to write their names with a few calligraphy techniques.

Arts/Crafts Experience

• Let students try the Middle Age craft of "quilling." They wrap thin strips of paper around a pencil and hold it for a few minutes to create beautiful curls that can be positioned in interesting designs on paper.

Extension Activities

• Host a Middle Ages Feast. Whatever you eat will have to be eaten without utensils (such was the order of the day). Try serving "finger food" such as cheese, hard rolls or pancakes to your class today!

Follow-Up/Homework Idea

• Remind students that since we are not in the Middle Ages anymore, they probably better return to eating with utensils at dinner tonight.

Middle
Ages

Middle
Ages

Middle
Ages

Long, Long Ago Day

September 12

Setting the Stage

• Display pictures of various time periods reflecting the course of human history around related literature.

• Often younger students do not have a grasp on the concept of time and its passage through history. Construct a semantic web with the things your students think of when you say the words, *long ago*. You might be surprised at how "short" *long ago* is to them.

Literary Exploration

About Doctors of Long Ago by Naida Dickson
Children of Long Ago by Lessie Little
How They Built Long Ago by Christopher Fagg
How They Lived in Cities Long Ago by R.J. Unstead
Let's Find Out About Animals of Long Ago by Martha Shapp
Living Long Ago: Homes and Houses by Helen Edom
Long Ago in a Castle: What Was It Like Living in a Castle? by Marie Farr
Long, Long Ago by Michael Berenstain

Science/Health Experience

• Learn about medical techniques from long ago by browsing through Naida Dickson's book *About Doctors of Long Ago*.

Social Studies Experience

- Learn about ancient architecture from Christopher Fagg's book *How They Built Long Ago,* or *Long Ago in a Castle: What Was It Like Living in a Castle?* by Marie Farre.

- Study significant events in world history and place them on a class time line. A good basis can be found from reading Michael Berenstain's book *Long, Long Ago.*

- Let students research historical events then share their information in five- to seven-minute oral reports.

Music/Dramatic Experience

- Borrow from your local library and play *Little Songs of Long Ago* by H. Willebeek leMair.

Physical/Sensory Experience

- Get some ideas for games from *Games from Long Ago* by Bobbie Kalman.

Arts/Crafts Experience

- Divide students into groups of different time periods. Let them create a mural about that special period of time (such as the 1700s or 1900s).

Follow-Up/Homework Idea

- Ask children to interview parents, grandparents or neighbors about something that has changed significantly during their lifetime. Have students report back to the class.

Roald Dahl's Birthday

September 13

Setting the Stage

• Display various selections from Roald Dahl's treasury of children's books.

Historical Background

Today marks the birthday of Roald Dahl, a children's author from England who was born in 1916.

Literary Exploration

The Best of Roald Dahl by Roald Dahl
Boy: Tales of Childhood by Roald Dahl
Charlie and the Chocolate Factory by Roald Dahl
Charlie and the Great Glass Elevator by Roald Dahl
Danny, the Champion of the World by Roald Dahl
Dirty Beasts by Roald Dahl
Enormous Crocodile by Roald Dahl
Esio Trot by Roald Dahl
Fantastic Mr. Fox by Roald Dahl
George's Marvelous Medicine by Roald Dahl
The Giraffe and the Pelly and Me by Roald Dahl
Going Solo by Roald Dahl
James and the Giant Peach by Roald Dahl
The Magic Finger by Roald Dahl
Matilda by Roald Dahl
Roald Dahl's Revolting Rhymes by Roald Dahl
The Witches by Roald Dahl
The Wonderful Story of Henry Sugar and Six More by Roald Dahl

Language Experience

• Let students brainstorm as many words as they can that rhyme with *Dahl* (pronounced "Doll").

Writing Experience

• Students might enjoy adding a different twist to the end of one of Roald Dahl's stories.

Science/Health Experience

• Review insect (and spider) life after looking at the interesting characters in *James and the Giant Peach* (Earthworm, Ladybug, Old-Green Grasshopper, Glow-Worm, Silkworm, Centipede and Miss Spider).

Roald Dahl
Roald Dahl
Roald Dahl

Arts/Crafts Experience

• Let students illustrate a scene from a favorite Roald Dahl book.

Extension Activities

• Serve sliced peaches or peach cobbler (in honor of *James and the Giant Peach*) or "Everlasting Gobstoppers" (a candy from *Charlie and the Chocolate Factory*) found in most grocery stores.

• Try some fun recipes from Roald Dahl's cookbook, *Roald Dahl's Revolting Recipes.*

Follow-Up/Homework Idea

• Encourage students to check out one of Roald Dahl's books to begin reading tonight.

Football Fever Day

September 14

Football
Fever

Football
Fever

Football
Fever

Setting the Stage

• Display football paraphernalia (football, pennants, helmet, pom-poms, etc.) to stimulate interest. Touchdown!

• Display pictures of football players around various book jacket covers with the caption: "TACKLE a Good Book!"

• Display a football player surrounded by footballs with students' names on them. Add the caption: "We're off to a great KICKOFF this year!"

Historical Background

Traditionally in America, this is football season! The game of football is said to have begun in Ancient Greece and Rome.

Literary Exploration

Baseball, Football, Daddy and Me by David Friend
Crusher Is Coming! by Bob Graham
The Dallas Titans Get Ready for Bed by Karla Kuskin
Dog for a Day by Dick Gackenback
The First Book of Football by John Madden
Football by Ray Broekel
Football Kids by George Sullivan
Football Legends by Bob Italia
Football: Start Right and Play Well by Bill Gutman
Football Talk for Beginners by Howard Liss
How to Star in Football by Herman Masin
It's Your First Kiss, Charlie Brown by Charles M. Schultz
Kick, Pass and Run by Leonard Kessler
Louanne Pig in Making the Team by Nancy Carlson
Miss Nelson Has a Field Day by Harry Allard
Sidney Rella and the Glass Sneaker by Bernice Myers
You Are the Coach by Nate Aeseng

Language Experience

• Illustrate (as a class) a Venn diagram that compares watching a football game on television versus attending a live game.

• As a class, brainstorm professional or other football teams, then have students alphabetize them.

• Construct a semantic map or web of things your students already understand about the game of football. Then list questions they have which will help you in your football emphasis today.

Writing Experience

- Let students write their predictions for an upcoming big football game (real or imaginary) along with their reasons for those predictions.

- Have students use their imagination to write about the time they were an "all-star at the Homecoming game!"

- Let students write about their feelings from a football's point of view. See reproducible on page 84.

Football
Fever

Football
Fever

Football
Fever

Football Fever!

Math Experience

- Create a "football field" on the board. Divide the class into two team[s] Let them name their teams. Give math problems (orally or on flash cards) for each team to complete. The team "huddles" together to decide on their team answer before giving it orally. The team that gives the correct answer gains yardage toward their goal. Interferenc[e] can be called for distractions. What a fun way to review math skills! Copy the football flash card below for your football math!

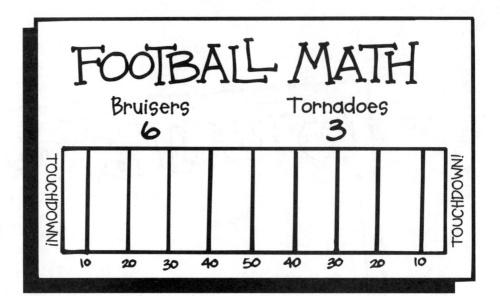

Science/Health Experience

• Review football safety.

• Keep your football field (from the Math Experience activity) on the board and ask science questions from your current science studies to play the game.

Social Studies Experience

• The football field on the board can also be used with trivia questions from history or current world social studies.

Music/Dramatic Experience

• Have students write a dialogue between a coach and a football player who made the winning touchdown or losing point in a game. They may act out the dialogue or turn it into a football "commentary" (seen on television) after a big game.

• Pantomime with your class basic football signals.

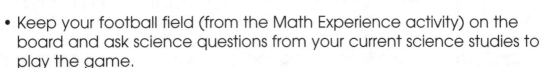

Football Fever

Football Fever

Football Fever

Physical/Sensory Experience

- Play a simplified version of Flag Football. Give each student a long piece of crepe paper for a "flag." They can put it in a back pocket or hold it in a hand trailing out for others to see. At your signal, everyone runs and tries to grab as many "flag tags" as possible. When the whistle is blown, tags are counted to see who has the most.

- How about a game of Football Pudding? Spoon ingredients of a chocolate pudding recipe into a clear, zip-type gallon plastic bag. Let students "play football" by tossing the pudding back and forth. Before long, the pudding will be mixed and can be chilled before eating.

Arts/Crafts Experience

- Students might want to make a papier-mâché football.

TLC10453 Copyright © Teaching & Learning Company, Carthage, IL 62321-0

Extension Activities

- Miniature "football" pies (made with fruit or meat filling) can be made by flattening refrigerator biscuit dough into two 4" circles. Spoon filling in the center of one circle, then top it with the other flattened biscuit. Students can shape the dough into football shapes and pinch them shut to seal the edges. The "footballs" should be baked in a 425°F oven for 8-10 minutes. Yummy!

- Invite a football player or coach to talk to your class about football and why it is so enjoyable.

Values Education Experience

- During the first professional football game, each player was paid $10. Compare that with what football players are paid now (some are reported to make over $125,000 per game). Discuss how high athlete salaries have become. What does this indicate about our current value system?

Football Fever!

Squirrel-y Skills Day

September 15

Setting the Stage

• Display pictures of squirrels or stuffed toy squirrels around related literature to get your students excited about the day.

• Display student work around an image of a squirrel with the caption, "We're Absolutely NUTS About Our Good Work!"

Historical Background

The Forest Service introduced a new character, "Woodsy Owl," in their campaign "Give a Hoot; Don't Pollute" to protect forest animals such as the squirrel.

Literary Exploration

Attila the Angry by Marjorie Weinman Sharmat
Beany and Scamp by Lisa Bassett
The Big Squirrel and the Little Rhinoceros by Mischa Damjan
Chessie the Long Island Squirrel by Sachiko Komoto
Erik Has a Squirrel by Hans Peterson
Ground Squirrels by Colleen Bare
Little Squirrel's Missing Seeds by Caroline Arnold
The Meanest Squirrel I Ever Met by Gene Zion
Merle the High Flying Squirrel by Bill Peet
Phewtus the Squirrel by V.H. Drummond
Scamper by Edna Miller
The Squirrel by Margaret Lane
The Squirrel in the Trees by Jennifer Coldrey
Squirrel Park by Lisa Ernst
Survival: Could You Be a Squirrel? by Fion Pragoff
The Tale of Squirrel Nutkin by Beatrix Potter
There's More—Much More by Sue Alexander

Language Experience

• Let students brainstorm other words that begin with "sq" as in the wor
  squirrel.

Writing Experience

• Have students write a paper on "Why I'm NUTS About Me!" See reproducible on page 89.

Name:

Why I'm **NUTS** about me!

Math Experience

• Let students use various types of nuts for math manipulatives or counters to practice counting, addition and subtraction skills. (Discourage children from eating these manipulatives.)

Science/Health Experience

• Learn about squirrels, chipmunks and other woodland creatures and their habitats.

Music/Dramatic Experience

• Sing the old Dutch folk song, "A Basketful of Nuts."

Physical/Sensory Experience

• Play the game, Squirrels in the Trees! Divide the class into groups of three. Assign each student in a group to be a "one," a "two" or a "three." Numbers "one " and "two" join hands to resemble a hollow tree that could house a lonely squirrel and number "three" is the squirrel. At the leader's signal, all squirrels run in search of a new home. There should be one extra squirrel who cannot find a home (much like Musical Chairs).

Arts/Crafts Experience

• Students will enjoy drawing a picture of a squirrel, cutting it into puzzle pieces, then letting other students try to assemble the puzzle.

Squirrel-y Skills

Extension Activities

• Serve a squirrel's favorite snack—seeds or nuts! (Be especially alert to any food allergies your children may have when serving nuts.)

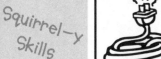
Squirrel-y Skills

Follow-Up/Homework Idea

• Explain to students that while many people enjoy the cute and clever antics of squirrels, others see them as pests. Ask students to survey friends and family as to their opinions of squirrels. Collect responses and publish the results.

Squirrel-y Skills

Why I'm
NUTS
about me!

Name:

Makin' Music Day

September 16

Setting the Stage

- Display pictures of performing musicians, as well as tapes, albums and CDs around tape recorders, a stereo or musical instruments to get you students in the mood for today's emphasis.

- Construct a semantic web of facts your students already know (or would like to know) about music to help structure your day.

Literary Exploration

The Boy Who Loved Music by David McPhail
Children's Songs by A.W. Hart
Kids Make Music!: Clapping & Tapping from Bach to Rock by Avery Ha
and Paul Mantell

Writing Experience

• Ask students to write about their favorite kind of music and the feelings they have when they listen to it. See reproducible on page 96.

My favorite kind of MUSIC!

Name:

Math Experience

• Play Musical Math! Put a math paper on each student's desk with sample math problems. As in Musical Chairs, they walk around when the music begins and when it stops, each one must stop in front of a desk and complete a math problem. Kids will love it!

Science/Health Experience

• Teach students correct posture and proper breathing when singing.

la, la, la, la

Social Studies Experience

• Learn about famous composers such as Bach, Handel, Hadyn, Moza Beethoven, Schubert, Tchaikovsky, Debussey, Copland, Bernstein and Ellington.

Music/Dramatic Experience

• Teach your students about: singing on pitch, rhythmic patterns of $^4/_4$ and $^3/_4$ time, how to identify accent and meter and how to recogniz when a melody is the same, steps up or down, or skips. Let them sing chants and rounds.

Makin' Music (appears in left margin)

92

Music/Dramatic Experience continued

- Create music with whatever you've got! A wooden spoon beat on an oatmeal canister or metal bowl can be a drum; bells attached around the edge of a paper plate can become a tambourine; paper plates filled with rice or dried beans, then taped together can be a percussion instrument; rubber bands stretched across an empty tissue box can become an instant guitar! Let students use their imagination!

- Let students experiment with making music their own way. Provide a blank tape and a tape recorder to record their efforts.

- Sing all the old favorites today! Don't forget such classics as "If You're Happy and You Know It," "Are You Sleeping?" "This Old Man," "I'm a Little Teapot," "I've Been Working on the Railroad," "The Ants Go Marching" and "The Farmer in the Dell."

- Borrow from a local library a recording of *We Are America's Children* by Ella Jenkins to play for your students.

Physical/Sensory Experience

• Let students experiment with the levels of water in eight tall glasses of
water to make the sounds of the musical scale: Do, Re, Mi, Fa, So, La,
Ti, Do. They'll also need a spoon or knife.

• Play Musical Papers. Instead of using chairs as in Musical Chairs, students stand on pieces of construction paper. Place the paper marke[r]
in a circle. Students walk around to the music. When the music stops,
each student stands on a paper. Each time a paper is taken away.
Students without papers are eliminated until there is only one student
left.

Arts/Crafts Experience

• Let students paint as you play various types
of music. Encourage them to
talk about how the music
makes them feel.

Extension Activities
- Let students make an edible flute by spreading peanut butter on a piece of celery and adding raisin flute keys.

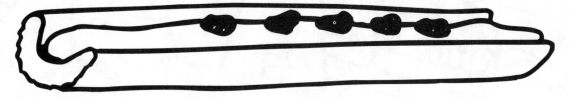

- If you have access to a musical production in your area, such as a local high school production, this would be a great field trip for your class.

Values Education Experience
- Discuss the value and importance of beautiful music to inspire, edify and uplift a person.

Follow-Up/Homework Idea
- Invite your students to listen to music at home that makes them feel good inside.

95

Name:

Constitution Day

September 17

Setting the Stage
- Display a copy of the U.S. Constitution with related literature to gather interest in today's activities.

- Construct a semantic web with everything your students already know (or would like to know) about the United States Constitution.

Historical Background
This week is officially known as Constitution Week because the U.S. Constitution was signed on this day in 1787.

Literary Exploration
Birth of the Constitution by Edmund Lindrop
The Constitution by Warren Colman
First Book of the Constitution by Richard Morris
A More Perfect Union: The Story of Our Constitution by Betsy Maestro
The Story of the Constitution by Marilyn Prolman
We the People: The Constitution of the United States by Peter Spier

Language Experience
• Challenge your students to see how many words they can make from the letters in the word *Constitution*.

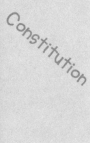

Writing Experience
• Create a class constitution. Involve everyone in a writing assignment about the rights and responsibilities of the students in your class entitle "We the People." Make suggestions, such as: the right for personal safety, respect for people's individuality, the right to have a voice in the classroom and the right to learn and be fairly treated. See reproducible on page 100.

We the people....

Name:

98

Social Studies Experience

- Give your students background information about the Constitution, the events leading up to it and the measures taken for its adoption. Discuss what the Constitution contains (responsibilities of the three branches of government, the relationship that states have to the federal government and how the Constitution can be amended (or have changes made to it).

- Let interested students do biographical research about framers of the Constitution, such as: Thomas Jefferson, Benjamin Franklin and James Madison. Have them share their information with the rest of the class.

Music/Dramatic Experience

- Borrow a sound recording from a local library of Janeen Brady's "Take Your Hat Off When the Flag Goes By."

Extension Activities

- Host a mock Constitutional Convention. Let students pretend to be delegates in Philadelphia, Pennsylvania, trying to agree on a common document in your classroom. Have them draft a document issuing the form of government your class will have, its responsibilities and the amendment process for your class constitution.

Follow-Up/Homework Idea

- Challenge your students to involve their families in a discussion about how rules of fairness and respect have been set up in their homes.

We the people....

Name:

Citizenship Day

September 18

Setting the Stage

• Display pictures of people doing nice things for their neighbors and communities. Arrange these around related literature.

• Construct a semantic web with words your students think of when you say the word *citizen*.

Historical Background

Constitution Week, celebrated September 17-23 of each year, has also been designated as Citizenship Week. Ordinary people around the world are recognized for doing good things in their communities.

Literary Exploration

Citizenship by Jay Schleifer
Citizenship: Learning to Live as Responsible Citizens by Debbie Pincus
Let's Find Out About the Community by Valerie Pitt
What Is a Community? by Carole Bertol

Language Experience

• Let students brainstorm words that describe a good citizen (hard-work-ing, honest, helpful, respectful). Then have them arrange the words in alphabetical order.

Writing Experience

• Give students time to write what they think constitutes a good citizen and how they see themselves in that light. See reproducible on page 104.

What is a good CITIZEN?

Name:

102

Music/Dramatic Experience

• Have students role-play how they could model good citizenship (helping an older person struggle with grocery packages, etc.).

Arts/Crafts Experience

• Let students draw pictures or create a mural of people doing nice things in their community.

Extension Activities

• Invite a local community leader to speak to your class on the importance of citizens working together for the good of the community.

Follow-Up/Homework Idea

• Encourage students to look for ways to become better citizens as they go home (picking up litter, opening a door for someone, etc.).

What is a good CITIZEN?

Name:

Mapping Madness Day

September 19

Setting the Stage

- Display a map as a backdrop or bulletin board background.

- Check with a local automobile club to see if they have extra maps to donate to your class.

- Construct a semantic "map" with everything your students know (or want to know) about maps and how they work.

Historical Background

The Montgolfier brothers sent up their hot air balloon with its first passengers (duck, sheep and rooster) on this day in 1783. I wonder if they had a map?

Mapping
Madness

Mapping
Madness
Mapping
Madness

Literary Exploration

Fergus and Bridey by Oliver Dunrea
Geography from A to Z: A Picture Glossary by Jack Knowlton
Git Along, Old Scudder by Stephen Gammell
Maps and Globes by Ray Broekel
Maps and Globes by Jack Knowlton
Maps and Maps by Barbara Taylor
A Map Is a Picture by Barbara Rinkoff
Me on the Map by Joan Sweeney
My Map Book by Sara Fanelli
What Is Beyond That Hill? by Ernst Ekker
What's in a Map? by Sally Cartwright

Language Experience

• Let students brainstorm words that rhyme with the word *map*.

Social Studies Experience

• Today is a perfect opportunity to begin a unit on mapping skills.

• Help students remember the cardinal directions (North, East, South and West) by remembering (N.E.S.W.—"Never Eat Soggy Worms" (or "waffles" for the faint of heart).

Physical/Sensory Experience

- Give students an opportunity to have "hands-on" experience with how a map works. Provide blocks, cubes or paper tubes to represent desks and other objects in your classroom. Students should try to manipulate the items as they might look on a paper map before actually drawing one with paper and pencil.

Arts/Crafts Experience

- Let students draw a map (with a key) of your school or neighborhood. Save the maps to give new students or kindergarteners to help them find their way around unfamiliar territory.

- Move the desks aside and let students create a map of the world on the floor. Divide them into groups and make each group responsible for a specific area of the world.

Extension Activities

• Draw a map of your school (your principal may already have one) and make a key in the bottom corner that shows distinguishing areas (drinking fountain, fire extinguisher, heaters or a picture of a famous person). Send students on a scavenger hunt to find certain areas around the school using the school map. Have them color the areas on the map as they find them.

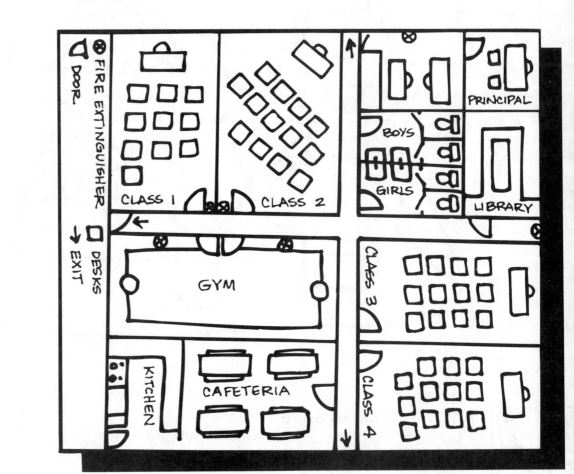

• Invite each student to create a map (using geography terms) of an imaginary country.

Follow-Up/Homework Idea

• Have students take a simple map of the United States home and go on a label hunt in their kitchens! They read labels on canned goods and commercial products to see where they were produced, then draw a little icon or symbol representing each item at the correct spot on the map.

Harvesttime Day

September 20

Setting the Stage

- Display students' work around harvest vegetables and fruits with the caption, "Cream of the Crop!" or "Harvesting Great Work!"

- Display a large bowl of fresh fruits and vegetables around related literature to provide the needed stimulus for today's activities.

- Construct a semantic web with words your students think of when you say the word *harvest*.

Historical Background

It's the time of year when gardens bring forth their bounties! Today we celebrate fall's harvest!

Literary Exploration

And So My Garden Grows by Peter Spier
Autumn Harvest by Alvin Tresselt
Bunnicula by Deborah and James Howe
Celie and the Harvest Fiddler by Valerie Flournoy
A Garden Is Good by Lillie D. Chaffin
Garden Partners by Diane Palmisciano
Grandpa's Garden Lunch by Judith Caseley
Grandpa's Too Good Garden by James Stevenson
Growing Vegetable Soup by Lois Ehlert
Hard Scrabble Harvest by Dahlov Zorach Ipcar
Harvest Feast by Wilhelmina Harper
Harvest Song by Ron Hirschi
Moose in the Garden by Nancy White Carlstrom
My Garden Grows by Aldren Watson
Seeds and More Seeds by Millicent E. Selsam
The Trouble with Grandad by Babette Cole
The Turnip by Janina Domanska
Two Little Gardeners by Margaret Wise Brown
Vegetable Garden by Douglas Florian
Vegetables by Susan Wake
Vegetable Soup by Jeanne Modesitt
We Celebrate the Harvest by Bobbie Kalman

Language Experience

• Students can brainstorm as many different vegetables as they can think of, then put them in alphabetical order.

Writing Experience

• Let students write about their favorite harvest foods. Ask them to describe how they look, smell and taste (using as much descriptive imagery as possible). See reproducible on page 114.

• Let students plan a harvest menu! Invite them to write a nutritious dinner menu using a variety of fresh vegetables and fruit.

I love VEGGIES!

Name: _____

110

Science/Health Experience

- Today is a perfect day to review planting, nurturing and harvesting crops.

- Have students plant parsley, tomato or radish seeds in milk carton halves.

- Review nutrition basics with your students as you talk about the nutritional value of fruits and vegetables, especially fresh from the garden.

Social Studies Experience

- Study some of the festivals honoring this time of year with Judith Corwin's book *Harvest Festivals Around the World*.

Physical/Sensory Experience

- Teach students how to recognize a fruit vegetable (such as a tomato), a root or tuberous vegetable (such as a potato) and a leafy vegetable (such as lettuce). Let them examine vegetable parts in a pea pod and take other vegetables apart to see where the seeds are. Leave them on the science table with a magnifying glass for further study. Compare frozen and canned vegetables with fresh ones. Let students note any differences in color or texture.

Arts/Crafts Experience

- Students will enjoy dipping cut vegetables into paint and pressing them onto paper to make vegetable prints.

- Students can be taught about the concept of "still life" art with a fruit and vegetable arrangement. Let them paint or draw with colored chalk what they see.

- Show students how to make a Vegetable Man! Draw a figure with carrots (legs), potato (lower half), cabbage (upper torso), yellow squash (arms and hands), beet (head) and a green pepper (hat or hair). Have them copy it or come up with their own ideas.

Extension Activities

- After reading Deborah and James Howe's book, *Bunnicula*, serve Bunnicula's all-white vegetable salad (peeled apples, mini marshmallows, cauliflower bits and celery mixed with whipped topping).

- Let students eat the different parts of plants: root (carrot, radish or turnip), stem (celery or green onion), leaf (lettuce, cabbage, parsley or watercress) and flowers (broccoli or cauliflower).

- If your school is near a grocery store, take your class on a field trip to the produce section and have them make observational drawings of the vegetables in season.

- Schedule a visit with a local gardener to see his harvest crops and hear him explain the process involved in growing fruits and vegetables.

Follow-Up/Homework Idea

- Remind students to eat all their vegetables (even lima beans) at dinner tonight!

I love VEGGIES!

Name: _____

First Day of Autumn

September 21

Setting the Stage

• Display student work around a paper tree with falling leaves and the caption, " 'Tree'mendously Good Work!" Adding a real leaf border can enhance this bulletin board idea even more. Lay leaves between sheets of wax paper (and colored tissue) and iron to seal the edges. Beautiful effect!

Historical Background

Traditionally, the first day of autumn (or fall) begins on this day each year. Sometimes it lands on September 22nd or 23rd (depending on the autumnal equinox).

Autumn

Literary Exploration

An Autumn Tale by David Updike
Autumn by Fiona Pragoff
Autumn by Ruth Thomson
Autumn Story by Jill Barklem
The Bear's Autumn by Keizaburo Tejima
The Cinnamon Hen's Autumn Day by Sandra Dutton
Cranberry Autumn by Wende Devlin
Dragon Kite of the Autumn Moon by Valerie Reddix
Every Autumn Comes the Bear by Jim Arnosky
A Harvest by Alvin Tresselt
Leaves by Fulvio Testa
Max and Maggie in Autumn by Janet Craig
Raking the Leaves with Max by Hanne Turk
Red Leaf, Yellow Leaf by Lois Ehlert
Say It! by Charlotte Zolotow
What Happens in Autumn? by Suzanne Venino
When Autumn Comes by Robert Maass
Where Do All the Birds Go? by Tracey Lewis

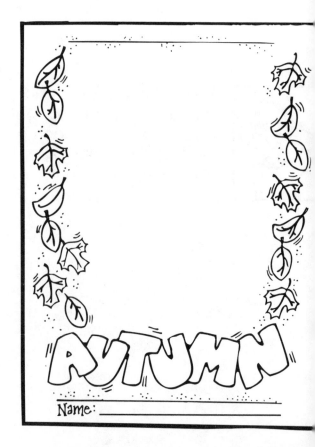

Autumn

Language Experience

• How many words can your students think of that rhyme with the word *fall*?

Writing Experience

• Let students write about the things they look forward to as the days get cooler. Add their writing to the bottom of a picture of autumn. See reproducible on page 121.

Autumn

116

Math Experience

• Let students graph on a bar graph various colors of leaves they find.

Science/Health Experience

• Discuss why some leaves change color and fall while others stay green and remain on the branches all year long. Explain how the pigment contained in the leaves determines their color. As it becomes cooler, some trees stop their flow of chlorophyll and the green pigment breaks down. All we see are the colors that remain. As the other pigment colors dry up, the leaves fall off the branches.

• Teach your students how to dissect and identify the parts of a leaf (stipule, stem, blade and veins).

Social Studies Experience

- Before there were calendars, farmers divided the year into parts whe[re] they could perform certain farm labors. At the fall equinox there are equal hours of night and day (12 hours each). Explain that from this day on (at least for the next few months) days will gradually get short[er] and nights will get longer. This is when animals start to hibernate and migrate.

- Learn about some autumn festivals around the world with Mike Rose[r] book *Autumn Festivals*.

Physical/Sensory Experience

- Go on a Leaf Hunt! Let students observe leaves that have fallen from the trees and those that are still on the branches. Show them decidu ous and non-deciduous (evergreen) leaves. Encourage them to gath[er] leaves. Later indicate the colors and kinds of leaves found on a class graph. See Math Experience on page 117. Maybe you can find leaf piles your students can jump in!

118

Arts/Crafts Experience

• If leaves have been collected, let students press leaves with a warm iron (with adult supervision) between two sheets of wax paper.

• Students will enjoy finger painting with fall colors on art paper. After the paint dries, they can trace leaf shapes over the painted background and cut them out to display around the room.

• Make leaf rubbings by letting students place a leaf under lightweight white paper and rubbing a crayon over it. The leaf (veins and all) should show through.

• Today would be a great day to teach students how to make a fall floral or leaf arrangement. To make an easy fall vase, have them dip small squares of colored tissue into a mixture of equal parts glue and water, then stick them on a soda bottle or old glass.

Extension Activities
• Take a fall nature walk and let your students draw the changes they see in nature at this time of year. They might want to gather items (such as acorns or seed pods) to form into a nature collage or add t the science table when they get back to class

Follow-Up/Homework Idea
• Encourage your students to rake their family's (or neighbor's) leaves a service project!

Name:

Pen Pal Day

September 22

Setting the Stage

• Set up a connection with another class or another school to begin a pen pal relationship. If you write to a school in another district or stat specify the grade on the envelope so that it gets to the right class. There are many resources available (some on-line) to help set up per pals for your class.

• Display examples of letters and postcards around related literature to create an environment for today's emphasis.

• Construct a semantic web with things your students already know (or want to know) about pen pals to help you structure your day.

Historical Background
The United States Post Office was established on this day in 1789.

Literary Exploration
Arthur's Pen Pal by Lillian Hoban
Harry's Smile by Kathy Caple

Language Experience
• Review the vowel sounds of short "e" and short "a" as in the words *pen* and *pal*. Let students brainstorm other words that contain those same vowel sounds.

Writing Experience

- Today is a perfect day to begin writing a pen pal from another class o another school. See reproducible on page 126.

- Review letter writing skills.

Dear Pen Pal,

Social Studies Experience

- If you can make a connection with another school in a different state (or better yet, in another country), invite students to suggest question to help them understand the other culture, educational experience way of life. Invite them to also share things about themselves: intere and hobbies, school, sports, family or friends. They may want to send school picture in the letter so the "pen pal" can visualize who is writin

Physical/Sensory Experience

- Encourage students to write legibly in their very best penpalship (penmanship).

- Blindfold one student at a time and play Pin the Stamp on the Envelope (a variation of Pin the Tail on the Donkey).

124

Arts/Crafts Experience

• Students will enjoy designing postcards to send to their pen pals. They can decorate one side and write a message and address on the other. See patterns on page 127.

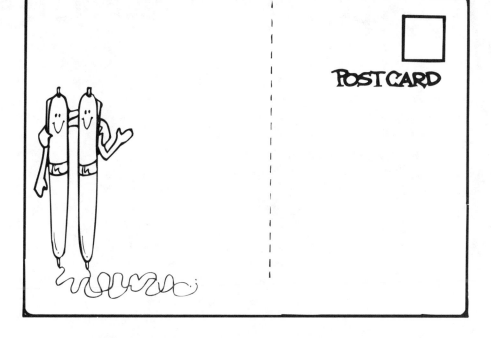

Follow-Up/Homework Idea

• Encourage students to be secret pen pals to members of their families, leaving special notes on pillows or dressers.

Dear Pen Pal,

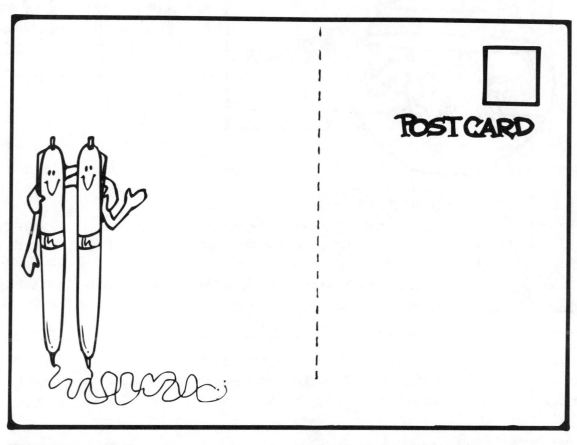

POST CARD

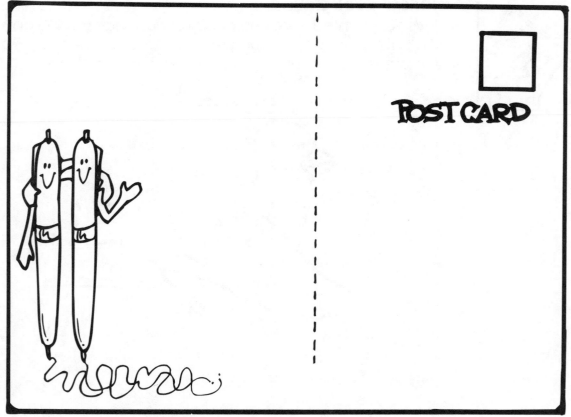

POST CARD

Pet Day

September 23

Setting the Stage

• Display stuffed animals and pictures of real pets around related literature to get your students excited about the day's activities.

• Create a bulletin board with pet care ideas written on various dog bone shapes and an image of a dog nearby with the caption, "BON Up on Your Pet Care Skills!"

• Construct a semantic web with everything your students already kno about pets. You'll be amazed at what they know! Then list students' questions about pets.

Historical Background

A dove was sighted from one of Columbus' ships (on this day in 1492), which gave them encouragement that land was nearby. Do you suppose a dove was one of the explorer's early pets?

Literary Exploration

Arthur's New Puppy by Marc Brown
Arthur's Pet Business by Marc Brown
A Bag Full of Pups by Dick Quackenback
Ben Finds a Friend by Anne Marie Chapouton
Capyboppy by Bill Peet
Emma's Pet by David McPhail
Esmeralda and the Pet Parade by Cecile Schoberle
Harry the Dirty Dog by Gene Zion
Hugo at the Window by Anne Rockwell
I Have a Pet! by Shari Halpern
I Love My Pets by Anne Rockwell
Incredible Journey by Sheila Burnford
Just Me and My Puppy by Mercer Mayer
Kitten for a Day by Ezra Jack Keats
Let's Get a Pet by Harriet Ziefert
Madeline's Rescue by Ludwig Bemelmans
Mouse Views: What the Class Pet Saw by Bruce McMillan
My Very Own Octopus by Bernard Most
No Mouse for Me by Robert Quakenbush
Old Yeller by Fred Gipson
Pet? by Ron Crawford
Pet Food by Jan Pienkowski
Pet Show by Ezra Jack Keats
A Pet to the Vet by Margaret Mahy
Plant Pet by Elise Primavera
The Puppy Who Wanted a Boy by Jane Thayer
Ribsy by Beverly Cleary
Rice Bowl Pet by Patricia Martin
See How They Grow: Puppy by Jane Burton
Socks by Beverly Cleary
Tenth Good Thing About Barney by Judith Viorst
When a Pet Dies by Fred Rogers
Where's Al? by Byron Barton
Where the Red Fern Grows by Wilson Rawls

Pets

Pets

Pets

Language Experience

- How many words can your students come up with that rhyme with the word *pet*?

- Create a Venn diagram depicting the likenesses and differences between cats and dogs.

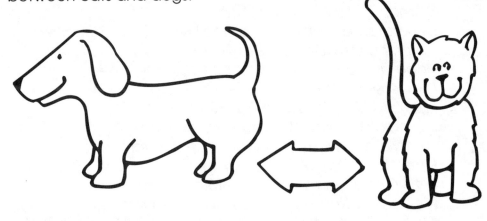

Writing Experience

- Give students an opportunity to write about "Life in the Doghouse" (a time when they found themselves "in the doghouse" and in trouble, or life from a "dog's-eye point of view"). See reproducible on page 136.

- Students may choose to write about one of these topics:
    The Unexpected Guest in My Dresser Drawer
    The Very Best Thing About Having a Pet
    If I Could Be a Pet I'd Be a _____ and I Would . . .

Pets

Pets

Pets

Math Experience

• When teaching missing addends, try this fun idea! Explain (in fun) that a big dog came and took a big bite out of part of the math problem and that the missing number is now a "soggy" number in a dog's mouth somewhere. Have students try to discover the mystery soggy numbers. (Example: 3 + __ = 7 means there is a soggy number 4 in some dog's mouth.) Your students will love it!

• Let students survey other students about their first choice for a pet. They can add this information to a class bar graph.

• Let students use dog biscuits for math manipulatives or counters as they practice counting, addition or subtraction.

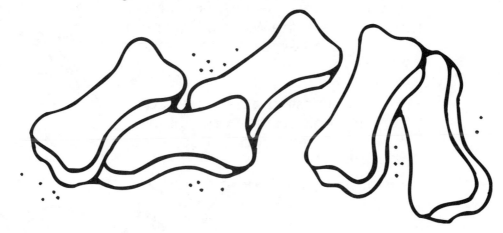

Science/Health Experience

• Today is a perfect day to begin a science unit on pet care.

• Study how pets differ: sleeping habits, body coverings, how they move (swim, crawl, run, fly).

Social Studies Experience

• Learn about pets around the world. Your students will be interested to know that a monkey might be a common pet in another country, or one might find a boy in another country walking a large iguana on a leash. Depending on cultures and what people are used to, pets are as varied as people.

Music/Dramatic Experience

• Sing the old favorite song, "How Much Is That Doggie in the Window?" (*Sharon, Lois & Braum's Great Big Hits*, Elephant Records).

• How about hosting a pet sound contest? Students can see who has the loudest, quietest, saddest, happiest or most unusual bark, meow, chirp or whatever!

• Set up your dramatic center to resemble a veterinarian's office with medical supplies (lab coat, stethoscope, etc.) and stuffed animals for your students to "treat."

Physical/Sensory Experience

• Play the old familiar Dog and Bone Game. One student is chosen to be the "dog" in front with his back to the class. A "bone" (eraser) is placed near him and the teacher selects another student to tiptoe near the "dog" to steal his "bone." If the "dog" hears that person and barks, he or she is caught and someone else tries. If the person is able to grab the bone without being heard, he or she becomes the new "dog." If the "dog" barks and no one is there, a new dog is chosen. This is a fun game for everyone!

Arts/Crafts Experience

• Students will enjoy painting or drawing their own pets (or dream pets).

• Students love making tactile pictures! Let each create an animal montage picture with items such as Shredded Wheat™ cereal to make a "bird nest" for birds; cornflakes to look like "leaves" on the trees with squirrels on the pretzel "branches"; seeds inside the centers of "flowers" with bees or hummingbirds flying by and fish-shaped crackers in a lake blowing Cheerios™ cereal "bubbles" in the water. Looks good enough to eat!

• Provide each student with a paper plate to fold in half. Have them add large wiggly eyes and other facial features (nose, whiskers, ears) and a big red construction paper tongue inside the paper plate "mouth." For an added touch, provide a rolled up piece of newspaper to be stapled inside the paper plate dog's mouth.

Extension Activities

- Call a local animal shelter to see if your class can "borrow" a pet for a trial period. Some shelters are willing to do this to provide educational experiences to local schools. Make sure you are aware of any pet allergies any of your students may have for this activity and those that follow.

- Host a Pet Show or Pet Parade! Invite students to bring in pets (real or stuffed). Let each share a little bit about the pet.

- If your school is near a pet shop, why not take your class there for a field trip?

Extension Activities continued

• Make a Puppy Dog Face Treat. Provide each student with a pear half for the head, a raisin for the eye, a prune for the ear, two mandarin orange slices for a collar and half a maraschino cherry for the nose to create an edible puppy dog face.

• Serve trail mix (or something similar) in round plastic bowls that resemble dog dishes.

• Invite a veterinarian to come and talk about his or her work with pets.

Values Education Experience

• Discuss the value in having a pet to love and care for, as well as to teach dependability and responsibility.

Follow-Up/Homework Idea

• Encourage students to take even better care of their pets (live or stuffed). Maybe they could host a birthday party for their pet!

Life in the doghouse

Name:

Native American Day

September 24

Native Americans

Setting the Stage

• Display various items that were introduced to us by Native Americans (turquoise and bead necklaces, leather moccasins, pottery, baskets, corn, squash and beans) around literature involving Native Americans.

Historical Background

The first observance of Native American Day was held in 1912. It is usually celebrated on the last Friday in September, a day set aside to honor and remember the culture and heritage of Native Americans.

Native Americans

Native Americans

Literary Exploration

Annie and the Old One by Miska Miles
Arrow to the Sun by Gerald McDermott
Buffalo Woman by Paul Goble
Ceremony: In the Circle of Life by White Deer of Autumn
Circle of Wonder by N. Scott Momaday
The Courage of Sarah Noble by Alice Dalgliesh
The First Strawberries: A Cherokee Story by Joseph Bruchac
The Gift of the Sacred Dog by Paul Goble
The Girl Who Loved Wild Horses by Paul Goble
Hawk, I'm Your Brother by Byrd Baylor
Iktomi and the Buzzard by Paul Goble
Itse Selu: Cherokee Harvest Festival by Daniel Pennington
Knots on a Counting Rope by Bill Martin, Jr.
The Legend of Bluebonnet by Tomie dePaola
The Legend of Scarface by Robert San Souci
The Legend of the Cranberry: A Paleo-Indian Tale by Ellin Greene
Many Winters by Nancy Wood
The Sign of the Beaver by Elizabeth George Speare
The Story of Sacajawea, Guide to Lewis and Clark by Della Rowland
The Tipi: A Center of Native American Life by David and Charlotte Yue
When Clay Sings by Byrd Baylor
Where the Buffaloes Begin by Olaf Baker

Writing Experience

• Let students write about the compelling plight of the Native American as others moved them more and more westward.

Math Experience

• Challenge your students to discover which coin honors the American Indian on one side and the buffalo (so important to the Native American way of life) on the other.

• Illustrate adding three or more addends, calling it Totem Pole Math. Show how to add each piece of the totem pole (and number) at a time.

Social Studies Experience

• Let interested students research various Native American tribes and their customs and be prepared to share their findings with the rest of the class.

Music/Dramatic Experience

• Borrow Charles Hofmann's *American Indians Sing* (a sound recording) or "Go My Son" (written by Burson-Nofchissey) from your local library to share with your students.

Physical/Sensory Experience

• Let students make up Native American tribal "rain" dances for fun!

• Set up a mock teepee in the room and let students have dramatic play fun dressed up as Native Americans.

• Check out from a local library Robert Hofsinde's book *Indian Sign Language*. Teach students some Native American sign language.

Native
Americans

Native
Americans

Native
Americans

Arts/Crafts Experience

• Students will enjoy creating shoe box dioramas with scenes depicting early Native American life.

• Give students an opportunity to make clay pots from modeling clay. They can make clay pottery by coiling bits of clay into ring shapes and layering one on top of the other.

• Construct a totem pole out of painted toilet paper tubes or thread spools.

• Let students try their hand at Navajo sand paintings. Use sand or salt mixed with dry tempera paint on a cardboard background. Mix equal parts of glue and water. Apply the glue mixture to the cardboard on any sketched design. Then sprinkle the sand or salt mixture onto the cardboard and it will adhere to the background. Shake off excess sand or salt and display!

140

Extension Activities

- Invite local Native Americans to come and talk about their culture and why they wish to preserve it.

- Enlist parent help in making Indian Fry Bread.

Indian Fry Bread

Mix: 2 c. flour, 1/2 c. powdered milk, 2 t. baking powder, 1/2 t. salt

Add warm water until mixture is the consistency of bread dough. Knead dough for 5 minutes. Let rise for 2 to 2 1/2 hours. Shape into balls and flatten into small circles. Poke a small hole in the center of each. Fry each piece in a shallow layer of oil. This needs to be watched carefully. After each piece of fry bread is golden brown on each side, let drain on paper towels and serve with honey or powdered sugar.

- Provide each student with a wooden skewer (used for small shish ke-babs) and let them arrange cut pieces of fruit in totem pole fashion for a fun treat!

Follow-Up/Homework Idea

- Challenge students to make an interesting Native American design with honey on bread for an after-school snack.

"Season"sationa Day

September 25

Setting the Stage

• Begin a bulletin board that can be kept up all year long. Display a large tree and make appropriate changes to it with each new season (fall: beautiful colors on the branches and some leaves on the ground; winter: snow all around with flaps that can be lifted to reveal hibernating animals; spring: buds on branches and baby animals and birds; summer: green leaves on the branches and children running through a sprinkler).

• Construct a semantic web with facts your students already know (or would like to know) about seasonal changes. This will help you plan activities for the day.

Literary Exploration

A Busy Year by Leo Lionni
A Child's Book of Seasons by Satomi Ichikawa
Fall Is Here by Jane Belk Moncure
Four Stories for Four Seasons by Tomie dePaola
Frog and Toad All Year by Arnold Lobel
My Favorite Time of Year by Susan Pearson
The Season Clock by Valerie Littlewood
Seasons by John Burningham
The Seasons of Arnold's Apple Tree by Gail Gibbons
Spring Is Here by Jane Belk Moncure
Summer Is Here by Jane Belk Moncure
When Springtime Comes by Ronnie Sellers
Winter Is Here by Jane Belk Moncure
Winter's Coming by Eve Bunting

Language Experience

- Have a spelling bee using the months and seasonal names of the year.

- Let students name the days of the week, months or seasons of the year and put them in alphabetical order.

Writing Experience

- Give students an opportunity to write about their favorite season of the year and explain why they like it best. See reproducible on page 145.

Math Experience

- Let students graph which months have 28 or 29, 30 and 31 days in them.

- Review calendar math (sequencing numbers on a calendar, tallying weekends or holidays).

Social Studies Experience

• Learn about the history of tracking time. Your students may not realize that centuries ago people watched the movements of the sun, moon and stars to record the tracking of time. Later Julius Caesar worked on creating a more uniform calendar that all could benefit from. In 1582 Pope Gregory XIII adjusted this calendar to what is known as the Gregorian calendar which is most widely used today.

Music/Dramatic Experience

• Play Seasonal Charades! Let students pantomime various activities, then let the class guess the appropriate seasons when they're done.

Arts/Crafts Experience

• Let students make homemade calendars today, and illustrate them with pictures that fit each month. See reproducibles on pages 146-15

• Have students make collages of seasonally appropriate activities.

Extension Activities

• Serve seasonal sweets! Let students taste items for each season (lemonade or ice cream for summer; apple cobbler or pumpkin pie fo fall; hot chocolate with marshmallows for winter; strawberry shortcake for spring).

Seasons

TLC10453 Copyright © Teaching & Learning Company, Carthage, IL 62321-0

My favorite SEASON

Name:

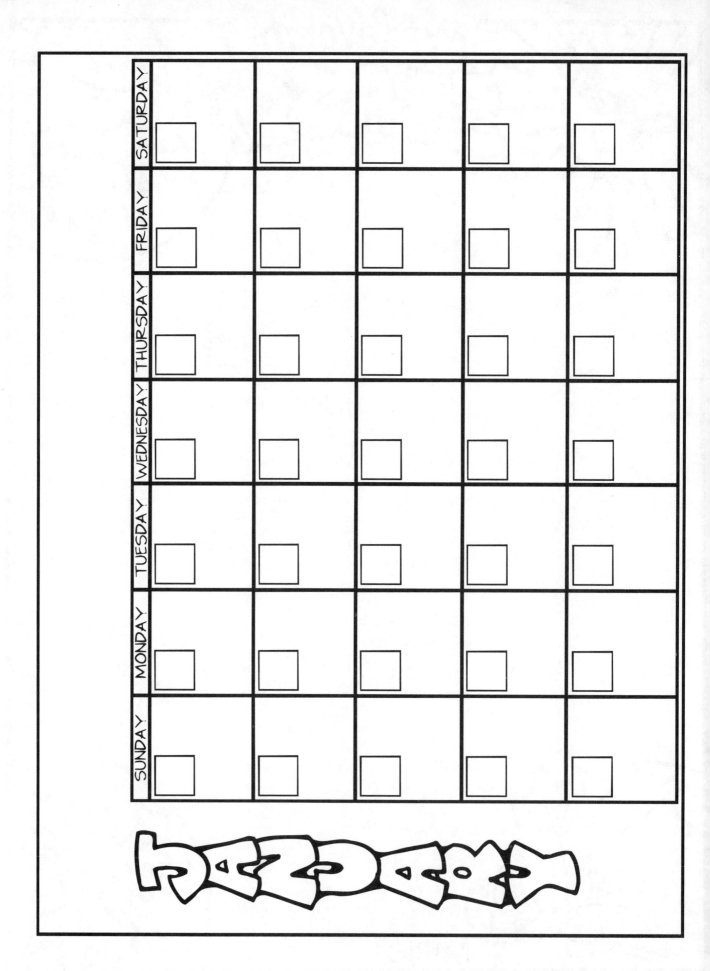

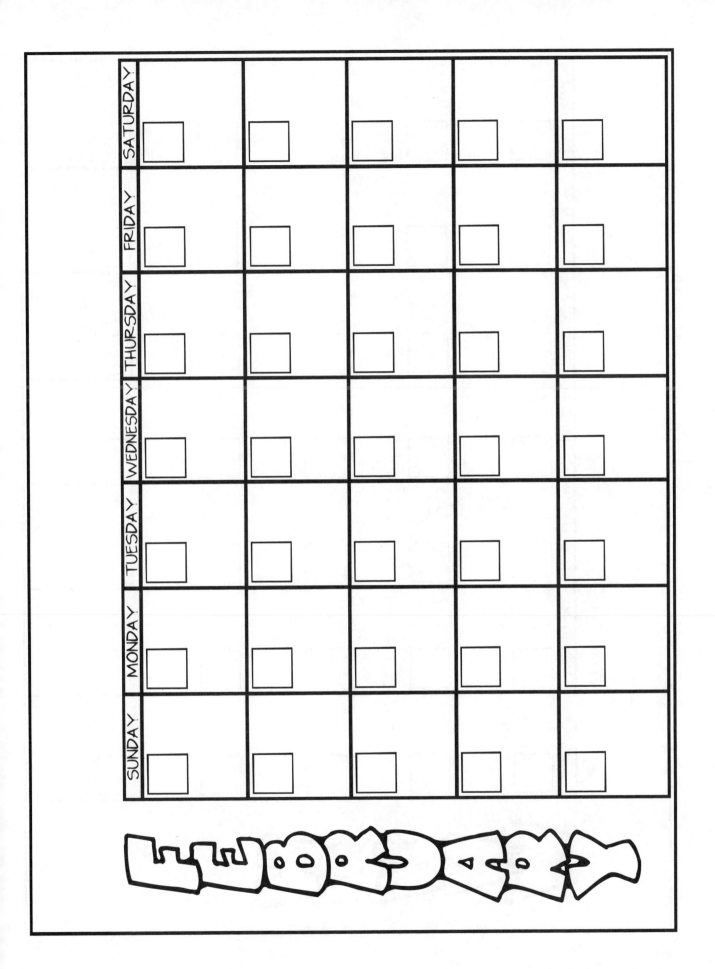

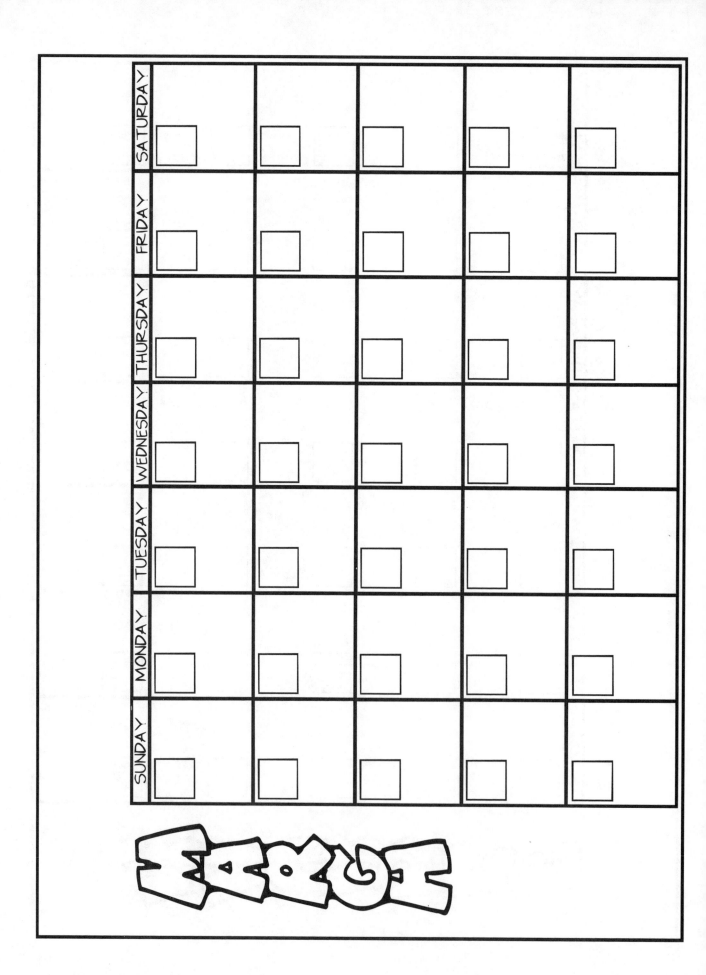

148

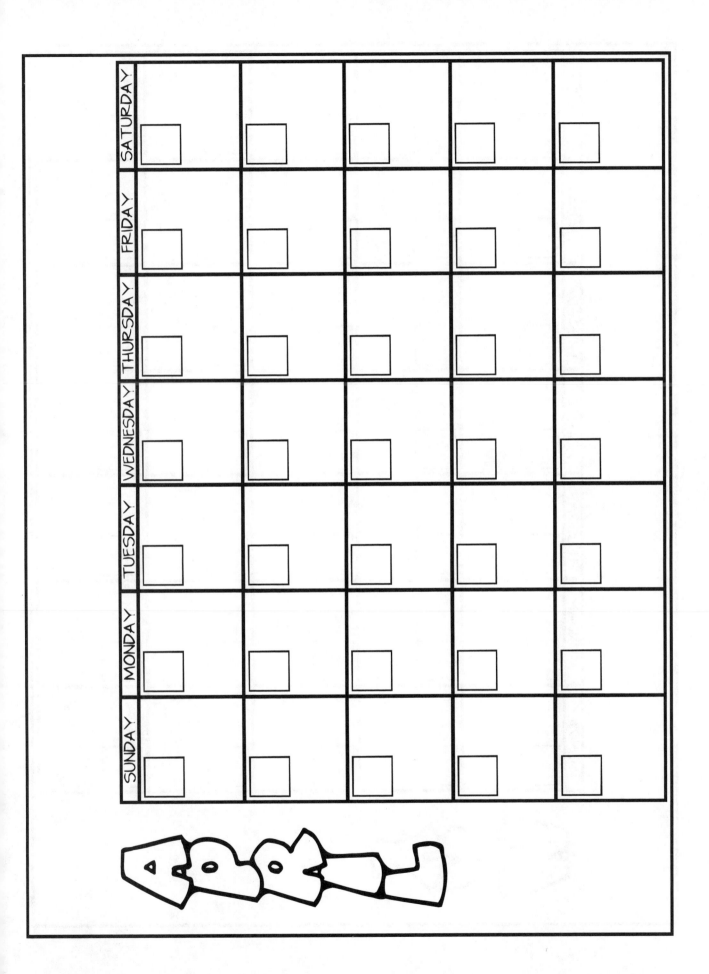

SUNDAY	MONDAY	TUESDAY	WEDNESDAY	THURSDAY	FRIDAY	SATURDAY
☐	☐	☐	☐	☐	☐	☐
☐	☐	☐	☐	☐	☐	☐
☐	☐	☐	☐	☐	☐	☐
☐	☐	☐	☐	☐	☐	☐
☐	☐	☐	☐	☐	☐	☐

150

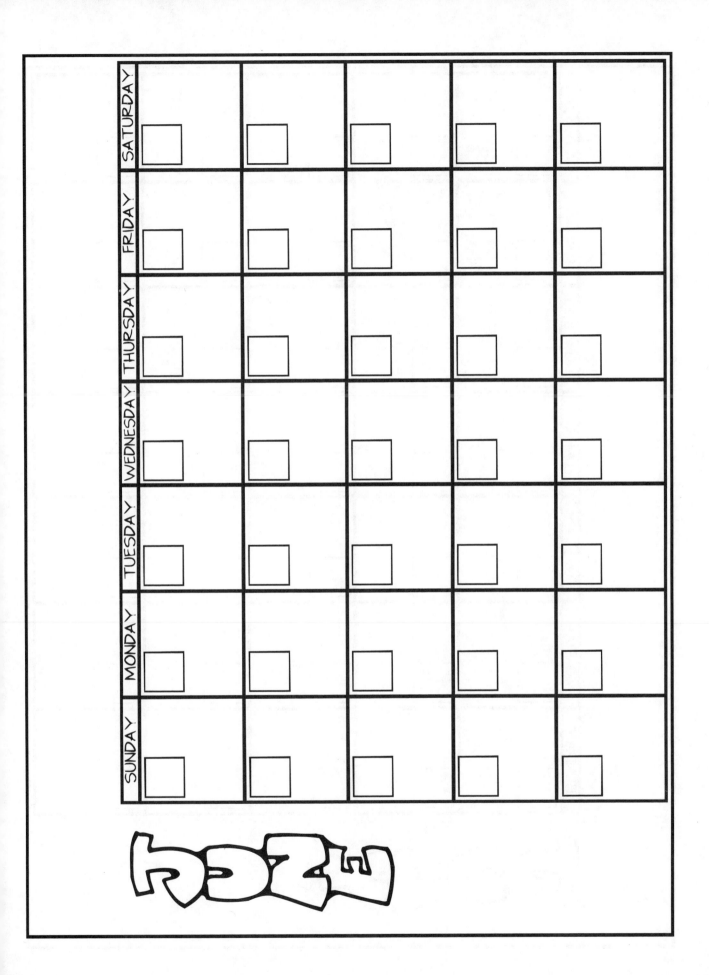

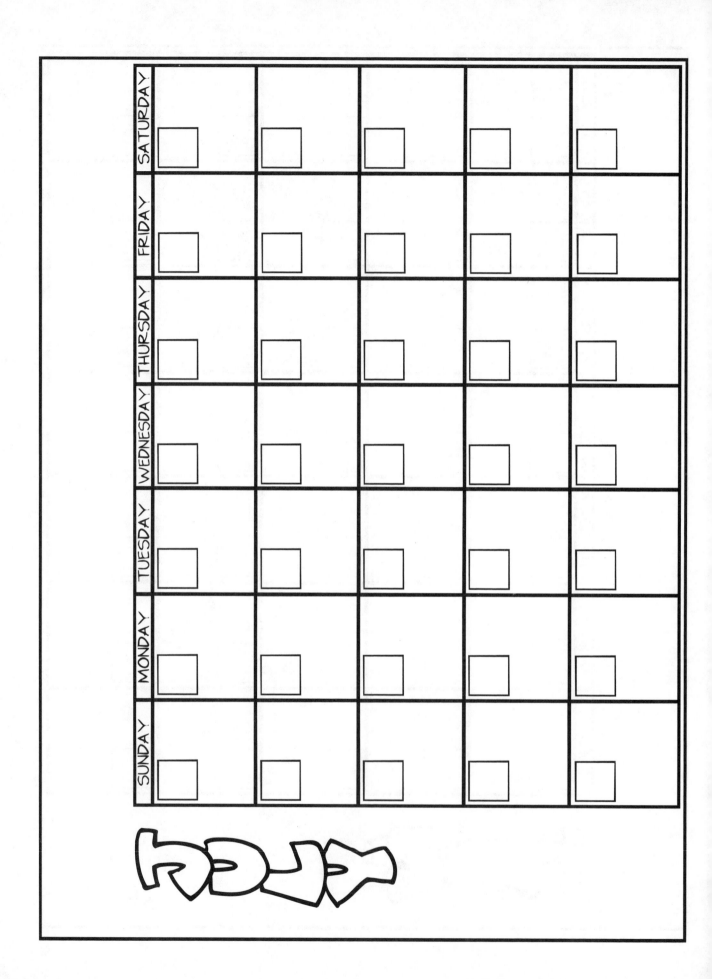

| SUNDAY | MONDAY | TUESDAY | WEDNESDAY | THURSDAY | FRIDAY | SATURDAY |

152

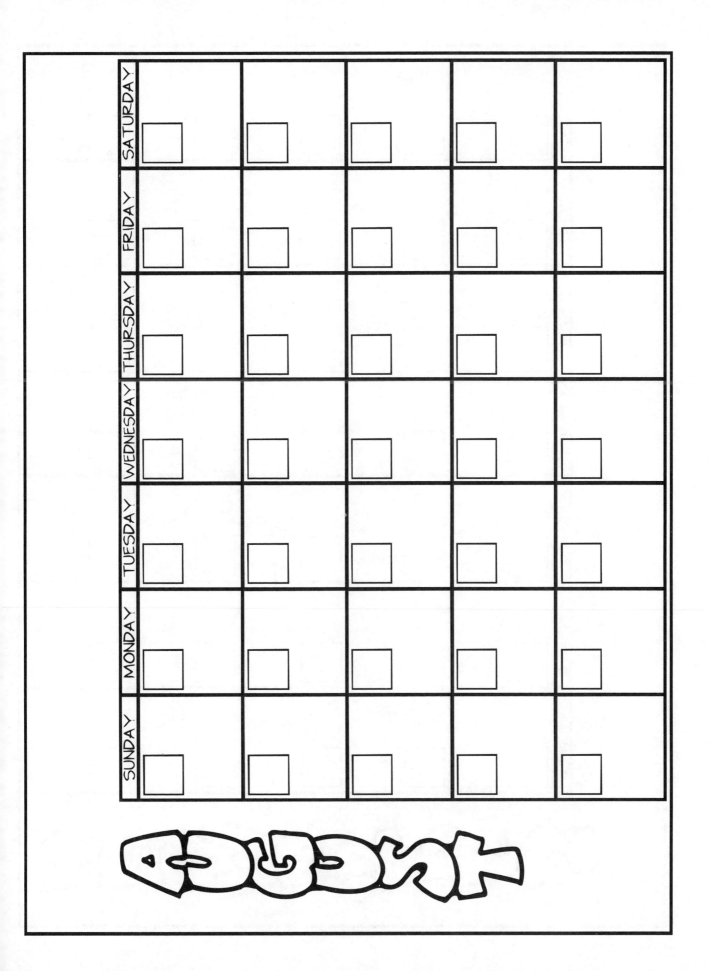

	SUNDAY	MONDAY	TUESDAY	WEDNESDAY	THURSDAY	FRIDAY	SATURDAY
	☐	☐	☐	☐	☐	☐	☐
	☐	☐	☐	☐	☐	☐	☐
	☐	☐	☐	☐	☐	☐	☐
	☐	☐	☐	☐	☐	☐	☐
	☐	☐	☐	☐	☐	☐	☐

SEPTEMBER

154

SUNDAY	MONDAY	TUESDAY	WEDNESDAY	THURSDAY	FRIDAY	SATURDAY
☐	☐	☐	☐	☐	☐	☐
☐	☐	☐	☐	☐	☐	☐
☐	☐	☐	☐	☐	☐	☐
☐	☐	☐	☐	☐	☐	☐
☐	☐	☐	☐	☐	☐	☐

OCTOBER

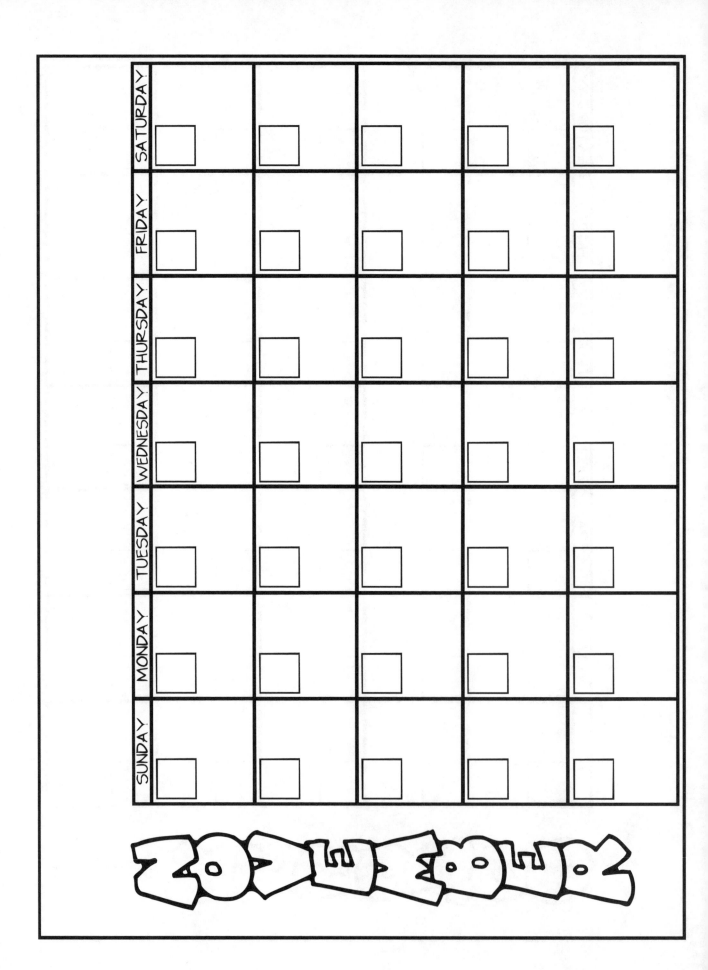

SUNDAY	MONDAY	TUESDAY	WEDNESDAY	THURSDAY	FRIDAY	SATURDAY
☐	☐	☐	☐	☐	☐	☐
☐	☐	☐	☐	☐	☐	☐
☐	☐	☐	☐	☐	☐	☐
☐	☐	☐	☐	☐	☐	☐
☐	☐	☐	☐	☐	☐	☐

COUNTDOWN

Johnny
Appleseed Da

September 26

Setting the Stage

- Display various types of apples and apple products around apple-related literature. If you decide to make applesauce (page 166), let simmer in a crockpot throughout the day. You will already have the students' attention!

- Many illustrations of Johnny Appleseed show him wearing a cooking pot on his head. Try greeting your students today with a pot on your head!

- Attach a large paper tree on a bulletin board. Cover the tree with student names or pictures on apple shapes. Add the caption, "You're the APPL of my eye!"

- Display book jacket covers around apple-shaped book reports that students have written with the ca tion, "Take a BITE Out of These!" or "Bite into a Goc Book!"

- Construct a semantic map or web with facts students know (or woul like to know) about apples or Johnny Appleseed.

158

Historical Background

John Chapman, who became known as Johnny Appleseed, was a pioneer and farmer born on this date in 1774. He became a folk hero as he made his way across America planting apple seeds. There is a park and other monuments honoring him near Fort Wayne, Indiana.

Johnny Appleseed

Literary Exploration

The Apple by Dick Bruna
An Apple a Day by Judi Barrett
An Apple a Day: From Orchard to You by Dorothy Hinshaw Patent
The Apple and the Moth by Enzo and Iela Mari
Apple Pigs by Ruth Orbach
Apple Tree by Barrie Watts
Apple Trees by Sylvia Johnson
Apple Valley Year by Ann Turner
Applebet: An ABC by Clyde Watson
Apples by Nonny Hogrogian
Apples, Aligators and Also Alphabets by Odette Johnson
Apples, Apples, Apples by Elizabeth Helfman
Apples, How They Grow by Bruce McMillan
How Do Apples Grow? by Betsy Maestro
I Can Read About Johnny Appleseed by J.I. Anderson
Johnny Appleseed by Jan Gleiter
Johnny Appleseed by Eva Moore
Johnny Appleseed by Gertrude Norman
Johnny Appleseed by Carol York
Johnny Appleseed: A Poem by Reeve Lindbergh
Johnny Appleseed: A Tale Retold by Steven Kellogg
Oats and Wild Apples by Frank Asch
Rain Makes Applesauce by Julian Scheer
The Real Johnny Appleseed by Laurie Lawlor
The Seasons of Arnold's Apple Tree by Gail Gibbons
The Story of Johnny Appleseed by Aliki
The Story of Johnny Appleseed by LaVere Anderson
Ten Apples Up on Top by Theo LeSieg (Dr. Suess)
The Value of Love: The Story of Johnny Appleseed by Ann Donegan
    Johnson
What Am I?: Looking Through Shapes About Apples by N.N. Charles
Who Stole the Apples? by Sigrid Heuck

Johnny Appleseed

Johnny Appleseed

159

Language Experience

- Read Steven Kellogg's book *Johnny Appleseed: A Tale Retold*. Disc[u] fact and fantasy regarding the life of Johnny "Appleseed" Chapma[n]

- Create a Venn diagram depicting the similarities and differences between apples and oranges.

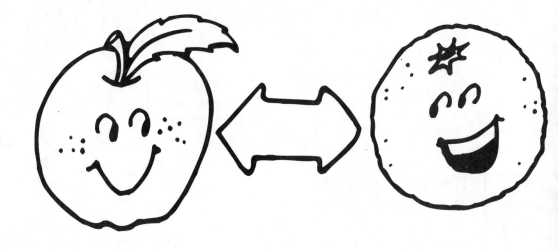

Writing Experience

- Johnny Appleseed planted apple seeds for others to enjoy (though h[e] would not reap the benefits) because he had a commitment to mak[-]ing the world a better place. Have students write about investments they would like to make for the future of others.

- Let students write about their favorite kinds of apples (tart or sweet; crisp or mellow; red, green or yellow) and their favorite ways to eat apples (fresh, caramel, baked, etc.). They may include their favorite apple recipes. See reproducible on page 168.

Johnny Appleseed

160

Math Experience

- Have students review fractions (halves, fourths or eighths) with apple sections, estimate seeds in an apple or apples in a bushel, sort and graph as well as review addition and subtraction skills.

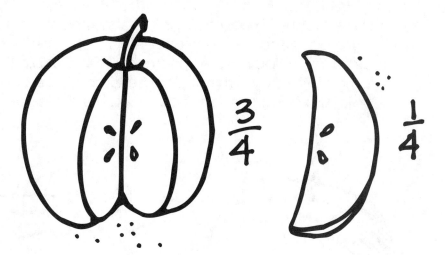

$\frac{3}{4}$ $\frac{1}{4}$

- Let students take a school or class survey of favorite kinds of apples. Show their findings with apple shapes on a class chart.

- Review place value with different colors of apples: yellow apples—hundreds, red apples—tens, green apples—ones place. Mix up various colors and amounts of each to reinforce this concept for a fun hands-on math manipulative.

Science/Health Experience

- Study the science of growing apples. Read *How Do Apples Grow?* by Betsy Maestro.

- Illustrate Sir Isaac Newton's experiment with gravity and an apple.

- Let students try to sprout some apple seeds. Record and illustrate changes each day.

Johnny
Appleseed

Johnny
Appleseed

Johnny
Appleseed

Science/Health Experience continued

- Discuss possible reasons for the old saying, "An apple a day keeps the doctor away." Do apples keep away sickness? Do your students th they will be healthier if they eat an apple every day?

- Experiment with peeled apples. What happens when the apples are exposed to the air? The oxygen in the air combines to turn the apple brown. Try dipping one in lemon juice. Explain that the one dipped lemon juice stays white because lemon juice contains citric acid wh acts as a coating substance much like the apple peel.

- Students can try dissecting an apple and making a diagram of its parts.

Social Studies Experience

- Do your students know that only about 20 of the over 7000 varieties apples are grown in the U.S.? Have them research other areas of th world where the climate is suitable for growing apples. (Hint: Apples can grow anyplace where summers are warm and winters are cold enough for trees to lose their fall leaves.)

- Study the life of John Chapman.

Music/Dramatic Experience

• Sing the song "Apples and Bananas."

Physical/Sensory Experience

• Let students bob for apples. Fill a tub or wide-mouthed bucket with water and add apples. Students put their hands behind their backs and try to grab an apple with their teeth.

• Younger students will enjoy pretending they are "growing" like an apple seed out of the earth.

• Let students balance an apple on a spoon or a cooking pot on their head while walking across the room. This is a great coordination exercise!

• Suspend apples from tree branches and let students, hands behind their backs, try to bite into the apples.

Arts/Crafts Experience

• Make apple prints. Cut apples in various shapes and sizes, dip them tempera paint and stamp out patterns.

• Students will enjoy making papier-mâché apples.

• Make wax paper apples! Let students shave red crayons with scissor onto wax paper. Top the wax paper with another sheet of wax pap Seal with a warm iron. When it's cool, students can cut apple shape from the wax paper to put on a bulletin board or decorate their app writing pages.

• Make shrunken apple heads. Peel and core apples. Cut slits for eye and mouth with scissors. Soak the apples for about 20 minutes in a mixture of water and two tablespoons of lemon juice. Take the appl out of the mixture and thread a pipe cleaner through the core, twisti the ends together. Hook this across a rope and let the apples dry fo few days. As the days progress, watch how the apple shrinks, addin character to the apple face. They can be skewered on a craft stick a puppet or taken home.

Extension Activities

- Cut two apple slices for each student, add peanut butter or honey to one side of each and sandwich the apples together like a pair of lips. Add mini marshmallows for "teeth" and you have a "mouth"-watering snack!

- A visit to an apple orchard would make a great field trip! Or take students to the produce section of a neighborhood grocery store to make observational drawings of the apples.

- Give each student an apple with a small hole scooped out and a gummy worm hanging out!

- Host an Apple-Tasting Party! Serve apple slices. Invite students to bring their favorite apple recipes (apple cobbler, apple pie, dried apples, apple butter, apple spice cake, apple juice). Use the apple recipes on pages 166-167 with your class.

Baked Apples

Core enough apples for each person and let them fill the center with brown sugar, cinnamon, raisins and nuts. Place apples in the bottom of a shallow baking dish with enough water in the pan to cover the bottom. Bake at 350°F for about 40 minutes.

Cool and serve with whipped cream!

Chunky Applesauce

Peel and slice about 8 apples. Put them in a crockpot with about 1½ cups water. Let apples slow-cook throughout the day. Add a little cinnamon and nutmeg as well as sugar to taste.

Enjoy warm or let it cool for a very tasty treat.

Apple Crisp

Mix ⅓ c. quick rolled oats, ¼ c. brown sugar, 3 T. flour, dash of salt and cinnamon. Mix with 3 T. butter. Peel and slice 4 or 5 apples and place in a shallow baking dish. Sprinkle mixture over apples and bake at 350°F for about 30 minutes.

After cooling, serve with vanilla ice cream or whipped cream.

Applesauce Slushy

Freeze applesauce ahead of
time in ice cube trays. Crush
in blender and serve.

Values Education Experience

• Discuss the saying, "One bad apple spoils the whole bunch."

Follow-Up/Homework Idea

• Thought-provoking homework question: "How many seeds in an apple
or how many apples in a seed?"

Name:

Folktales Day

September 27

Setting the Stage

• Set up various literary examples of folktales to get your students excited about the day's emphasis.

• Construct a semantic web with everything your students think of when you say the word *folktale*.

Literary Exploration

Agassu: Legend of the Leopard King by Rick Dupre
Best Loved Folk Tales of the World by Joanna Cole
Chicken Little by Steven Kellogg
The Children of Lir by Sheila MacGill-Callahan
Crow & Fox and Other Animal Legends by Jan Thornhill
Favorite Folktales from Around the World by Jane Yolen
Flossie and the Fox by Patricia McKissack
Folk Tale Plays Round the World by Paul T. Nolan
Mermaid Tales from Around the World by Mary Pope Osborne
Moon Magic: Stories from Asia by Katherine Davison
More Stories to Solve: 15 Folktales from Around the World by George Shannon
Mufaro's Beautiful Daughters by John Steptoe
One Hundred Favorite Folktales by Stith Thompson
The Shell Woman & the King: A Chinese Folktale by Laurence Yep
Song of Sedna by Robert D. San Souci
Sundiata: Lion King of Mali by David Wisniewski
Tales for Telling from Around the World by Mary Medlicott
The Talking Eggs by Robert D. San Souci
Three Wishes by Lee Peterson

Language Experience

• Introduce the literary genre of folktales. Explain to your students that folktales are legends or stories that have been handed down (told orally) from one generation to another.

Writing Experience

• Investigate with students the elements that make up folk and fairy ta[les] so they can write their own. A folktale usually takes place in a natur[al] istic setting while fairy tales most often take place in a supernatural s[et]ting. There is usually magic involved in the story with good triumphing over evil in the end. See reproducible on page 172.

Social Studies Experience

• Give your students a taste of the world through Joanna Cole's book *Best Loved Folk Tales of the World* or any of the other folktale selections in the list on page 169.

Music/Dramatic Experience

• Divide students into groups and let them perform short plays from Paul T. Nolan's book *Folk Tale Plays Round the World*.

Arts/Crafts Experience

• Let students illustrate a favorite folktale.

Follow-Up/Homework Idea

• Invite your students to check out a folktale to take home to begin reading tonight.

Good Neighbor Day

September 28

Good
Neighbor

Good
Neighbor

Good
Neighbor

Setting the Stage

• Obtain a city map that shows your school area with designated city streets. Place it on a bulletin board. Let students draw pictures of landmarks (school, stores, churches) on small pieces of paper. Attach pictures to the board and use yarn to connect them to the appropriate streets on the map.

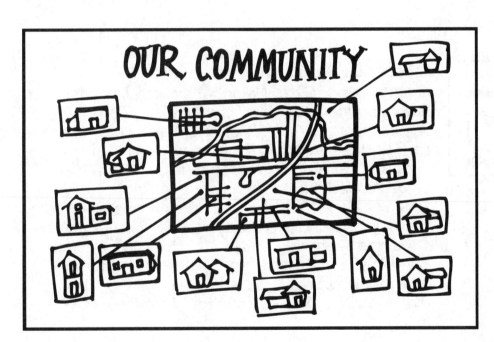

• Set up your classroom to resemble a neighborhood with city blocks and street names. Encourage friendship and teamwork to promote the feeling of "neighborhood" that can continue all year.

• Construct a semantic web with everything your students think of when you say the word *neighbor*.

Historical Background

Legend has it that a Greek soldier ran 26 miles (birth of the first maratho runner) to tell everyone the good news of the Persian defeat by the Greeks. What a neighborly thing to do!

Literary Exploration

Country Bear's Good Neighbor by Larry Dane Brimner
Harry and the Lady Next Door by Gene Zion
James Monroe's Good Neighbor Boy by Mabel Widdemer
Let's Find Out About Neighbors by Valerie Pitt
Let's Find Out About the Community by Valerie Pitt
Once Around the Block by Kevin Henkes
Susie & Alfred in a Welcome for Annie by Helen Craig
The Helping Hands Handbook: A Guidebook for Kids Who Want to Help
    People, Animals, and the World We Live In; Over 100 Projects Kids Ca
    Really Do by Patricia Adams and Jean Marzollo
Visiting a Village by Bobbie Kalman
Who Is My Neighbor? by Michael Grejniec

Language Experience

• Let students name community services in their neighborhood (airport, fire station, police station, hospital), then put them in alphabetical order.

Writing Experience

• Students can write thank-you letters to community helpers or neighbors who have been kind to them.

Social Studies Experience

• Today is a perfect day to begin a social studies unit on neighbors and communities.

• Review the roles of community helpers (firefighters, police officers, doctors, grocers, etc.). Let students make a chart listing community resources with phone numbers for easy access.

Music/Dramatic Experience

• Sing the Sesame Street song "The People in Your Neighborhood" (words and music by Jeffrey Moses).

Arts/Crafts Experience

- Provide large pieces of butcher paper for students to draw an aerial view of a model town.

- Let students create posters illustrating an act of neighborliness.

Extension Activities

- Host a Neighborhood Block Party! Invite "neighboring" classrooms to party with treats and games. Assign each class to be responsible for one item or activity.

Values Education Experience

- Long ago in the days of neighborhood barn raising, people depende on one another for mutual help and support. That interdependence created a sense of community. Encourage your students to continue that sense of community. Reinforce the importance of needing othe and the value of helping people.

Follow-Up/Homework Idea

• Give your students an opportunity to make a difference in their neighborhoods. Decide as a class what tasks they would like to do to help in their neighborhoods. List them for every student to copy. Make each task worth five points. See how many points students can earn. Students should go with adults or older siblings to complete the projects. Here are some suggestions:

Wash a window.
Roll up a garden hose.
Bring in someone's newspaper.
Play a simple game with a small child.
Pull 10 weeds.
Sweep off a porch.
Pick up 12 pieces of litter.
Sit and visit with an elderly neighbor for a few minutes.
Bring in someone's mail.
Read a short story to a child.
Take out someone's trash.
Water someone's plants.
Walk someone's dog.

Good Neighbor

Good Neighbor

Good Neighbor

Hippo Day

September 29

Setting the Stage

- Display pictures of hippopotamuses or any toy hippos next to related literature to get your students excited about the day.

- Construct a semantic web with all the facts your students already know (or would like to know) about the hippopotamus.

Literary Exploration

The Biggest Nose by Kathy Caple
But What Does the Hippopotamus Say? by Francesca Simon
George and Martha by James Marshall
Hank and Oogie by Nicki Weiss
Harvey, the Hiccuping Hippopotamus by Tanya Baker
Hiccup by Mercer Mayer
A Hippopotamus Ate the Teacher by Mike Thaler
Hippopotamus Hunt by Bernard Most
A Hippopotamusn't by Patrick Lewis
The Hippopotamus Song: A Muddy Love Story by Michael Flanders
Hot Hippopotamus by Hadithi Mwenye
Little Polar Bear by Hans deBeer
Our Ollie by Jan Ormerod
There's a Hippopotamus in My Bath! by Kyoko Matsuoka
There's a Hippopotamus Under My Bed by Mike Thaler
Think Hippo! by Wendy Smith
What Could a Hippopotamus Be? by Mike Thaler
What Should a Hippo Wear? by Jane Sutton
Where's My Hippopotamus? by Mark Alan Stamaty
"You Look Ridiculous," Said the Rhinocerous to the Hippopotamus by
    Bernard Waber

Hippos

Language Experience

• Challenge your students to see how many words they can make from
   the letters in the word *hippopotamus*.

Hippos

Science/Health Experience

• Learn about the hippopotamus and its habitat.

Hippos

179

Social Studies Experience
- With map in hand, locate places around the world where a hippopotamus might find its natural habitat.

Music/Dramatic Experience
- Sing J. Fred Coots' song "I Can't Spell *Hippopotamus*."

Arts/Crafts Experience
- Have students shape modeling clay into cute little hippos.

Extension Activities
- If your school is near a zoo, pay a visit to the lonely hippopotamus. His smell probably has something to do with his loneliness, but you've got to admit he's cute!

Rodeo Roundup Day

September 30

Rodeo
Roundup

Rodeo
Roundup

Rodeo
Roundup

Setting the Stage

- Howdy, Pardners! Get in the mood for a western theme today! Display cowboy paraphernalia surrounded by western-related literature.

- Display a paper cowboy with a lasso. Attach a real rope to the bulletin board around student names on excellent work samples or cowboy hats with the caption: "What a Roundup!" Or add western book jacket covers with the caption: "WANTED: Good Books. REWARD: Good Reading!"

- Challenge students to read with this bulletin board idea. Suggest that a student read every night with a parent for 20 minutes. Parents write their initials on a piece of paper and send it to school as proof. At school, students draw pictures of themselves horseback riding. Cut out the figures and place them inside a "corral" (roped area on a bulletin board). Each day students read, they get to keep their cowhands inside the corral. Those who remain in the corral throughout the reading challenge receive special certificates or privileges.

Setting the Stage continued

• Cover a bulletin board with WANTED posters. Have students draw self portraits. The class suggests captions to explain why they are "wanted" in the classroom. This is a great confidence booster! See reproducible on page 189.

• Dress like a cowhand (cowboy hat, bandana, chaps, jeans, spurs, big belt buckle, boots, bolero tie, etc.).

• Construct a semantic map or web with facts your students already know about cowboys, then list together what they want to learn about them throughout the day.

Literary Exploration

Armadillo Rodeo by Jan Brett

Bossy Boots by David Cox

The Brave Cowboy by Joan Walsh Anglund

Children of the Wild West by Russell Freedom

Cowboy Alphabet by James Rice

The Cowboy and the Black-Eyed Pea by Tony Johnston

Cowboy Andy by Edna Walker Chandler

Cowboy Country by Ann Herbert Scott

Cowboy Dreams by Dayal Kaur Khalsa

Cowboy Ed by Bill Grossman

Cowboy Rodeo by James Rice

Cowboy Small by Lois Lenski

Cowboys by Elaine Landau

The Cowboys by Leonard Mathews

Cowboys by Glen Rounds

Cowboys by Charles Sullivan

Cowboys of the Wild West by Russell Freedom

Cowgirl by Murray Tinkelman

Dakota Dugout by Ann Turner

Eyewitness Books: Cowboy by David M. Murdoch

Fact or Fiction: Cowboys by Stewart Ross

Four Dollars and Fifty Cents by Eric A. Kimmel

Go West, Swamp Monsters by Mary Blount Christian

I Want to Be a Cowboy by Liza Alexander

Jalapeno Hal by Jo Harper

Junior Rodeo by Anabel Dean

Let's Rodeo by Charles Coombs

Little Britches Rodeo by Murray Tinkelman

The Magic Boots by Scott Emerson and Howard Post

Matthew, the Cowboy by Ruth Hooker

Meanwhile Back at the Ranch by Trinka Hakes Noble

Pecos Bill by Ariane Dewey

Pecos Bill by Steven Kellogg

Ride 'Em Cowgirl by Lynn Haney

Rodeo by Cheryl Walsh Bellville

Rodeo Day by Jonelle Toriseva

Rodeo Horses by Candice Tillis Philp

Rodeos by James Fain

Rodeo School by Ed Radlauer

Rosie and the Rustlers by Roy Gerrard

Round-Up by Cheryl Walsh Bellville

Someday Rider by Ann Herbert

The Story of Nat Love (Stories of the Forgotten West) by Robert H. Miller

Tex, the Cowboy by Sarah Garland

White Dynamite and Curly Kidd by Bill Martin

Why Cowboys Sleep with Their Boots On by Laurie Lazzaaro

The Zebra-Riding Cowboy by Angela Shelf Medearis

Rodeo Roundup

Rodeo Roundup

Rodeo Roundup

Language Experience

• Review fact or fiction elements after reading *Fact or Fiction: Cowboy* by Stewart Ross.

Writing Experience

• This would be a great day to introduce students to writing adventure stories.

Math Experience

• Measure "lassos" (see Arts/Crafts Experience, page 187).

• Experiment with an old hat to see how much a 10-gallon hat really holds (Hint: less than one gallon).

Social Studies Experience

• Research the advent of the American cowboy in the west. Most cowboys had their heyday during a 30-year period after the Civil War. Have students make a time line of significant events.

• Let students do individual research on real Old West personalities: Buffalo Bill, Jesse James, Annie Oakley, Billy the Kidd, Wyatt Earp, Butch Cassidy, Calamity Jane, Wild Bill Hickok. Let them share their findings with the rest of the class.

Music/Dramatic Experience

• Sing old cowboy songs such as: "Home on the Range," "On Top of Old Smokey" and "Streets of Laredo." Local libraries are a great resource for Western music such as Alan Axelrod's *Songs of the Wild West*.

Physical/Sensory Experience

- Borrow a real saddle to place on a sawhorse. With adult help, studer can climb on the saddle and try to "lasso" a stationary object with a rope.

- Play Cowboy, Cowboy, Sheriff! (a variation of Duck, Duck, Goose). When the student who is "it" taps someone and says, "Sheriff," the sheriff chases the cowboy to put him in "jail" (the center of the circle) If the sheriff does not catch the cowboy, he has to go to jail instead.

- Conduct old-fashioned arm wrestling between interested students.

- Teach students a few basic square dancing steps such as "The Virginia Reel."

- Teach students basic knot-tying techniques, skills that cowboys of the Old West needed to know.

TLC10453 Copyright © Teaching & Learning Company, Carthage, IL 62321-C

Arts/Crafts Experience

- Make cowboy vests out of large grocery sacks. After cutting neck and armholes to fit, students cut a fringe at the bottom of the vest, then use markers and glitter for finishing touches!

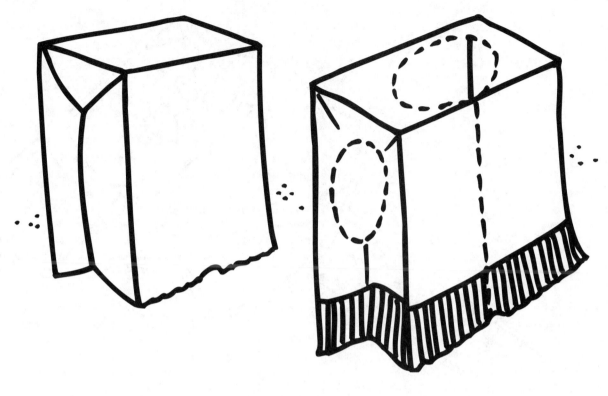

- Students can make their own bandanas out of red tissue paper. They simply fold a large square corner to corner to make a triangle and secure it loosely around the collar.

- These lassos will be a surefire hit! Cut a long piece of crepe paper (2" by $1\frac{1}{2}$' to 2') for each student. Fold a sheet of construction paper until it is about a 2" x 2" square. Place the end of the crepe paper in it and tape it closed with masking tape. Cut a piece of yarn (about 15" long). Wrap one end of the yarn around the construction paper square and tape it. In a gym or outside, students may whip their "lassos" around like ropes.

Arts/Crafts Experience continued

• Every cowpoke needs a horse! Students can make stick horses by tracing a horse head on both sides of a brown grocery sack and stuffing it for a three-dimensional effect. Before stapling the opening, stick a ruler through it for a handle. See patterns on pages 190 and 19

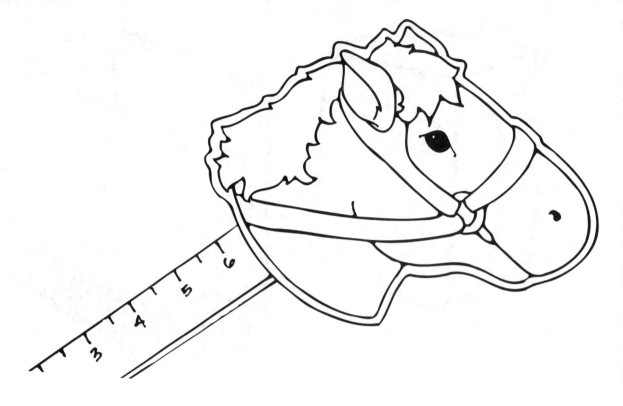

Extension Activities

• Construct a mock campfire (from construction paper "logs" and red plastic wrap "flames"). Serve pork and beans or chili beans in small cups (or pot pie tins), sarsaparilla (root beer) and "trail" mix!

• Invite someone who plays the guitar to play a few Western songs for a cowboy sing-along!

• Shape your favorite sugar cookie recipe into horseshoes and bake according to the recipe for a tasty treat!

• Invite someone who has ridden in a rodeo to share the experience with the class.

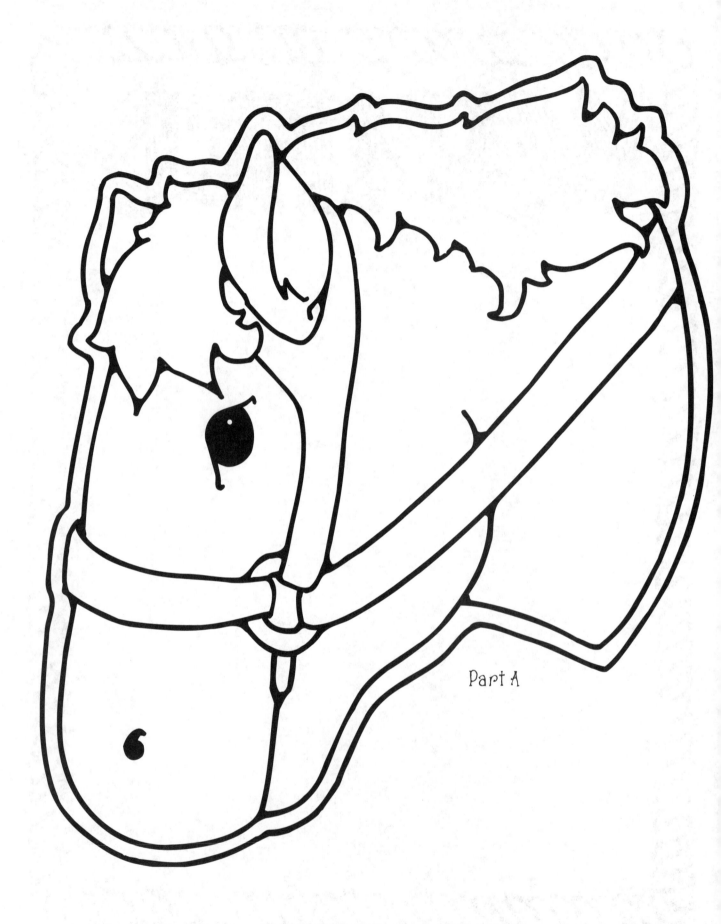

Part A

190

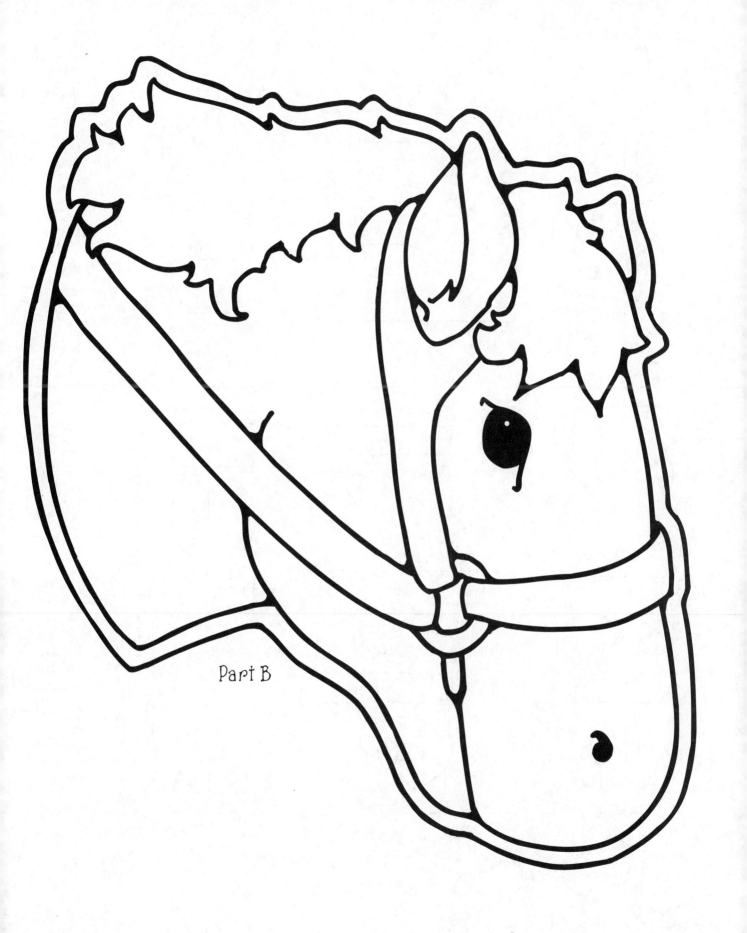

Part B

September

September

September

September